Items should be returned on or before the last date shown below. Items not already requested by other borrowers may be renewed in person, in writing or by telephone. To renew, please quote the number on the barcode label. To renew online a PIN is required. This can be requested at your local library.
Renew online @ **www.dublincitypubliclibraries.ie**
Fines charged for overdue items will include postage incurred in recovery. Damage to or loss of items will be charged to the borrower.

Leabharlanna Poiblí Chathair Bhaile Átha Cliath
Dublin City Public Libraries

Dublin City
Baile Átha Cliath

PEARSE STREET BRANCH
BRAINSE SRÁID PIARSACH
TEL. 6744888

Date Due	Date Due	Date Due
FEB 13 09 APR 2017		1 1 OCT 2018

D1375477

Trapattoni celebrates his 70th birthday, supervised by an interesting photo of Irish soccer manager legend Jack Charlton.
Credit: John Barrington/nineteen21

'I always say that in addition to being a coach, I'm also a priest. I go to each player's room and say who is playing and who isn't. I talk and explain. It's a little like confession.'

(Giovanni Trapattoni)

The Irish Fan's Guide to Euro 2012

Damien Moran

ORPEN PRESS

Orpen Press
Lonsdale House
Avoca Ave
Blackrock
Co. Dublin
Ireland

e-mail: info@orpenpress.com
www.orpenpress.com

ISBN 978-1-871305-55-5

Printed in the UK by MPG Ltd.

Questions or requests for more tips about Poland/Ukraine Euro
2012 or feedback to the author is very welcome. Please send to:
dbamoran@yahoo.com.

Official Anthem of the Irish Team for Euro 2012

Dublin singer-songwriter Damien Dempsey put together the 'Rocky Road to Poland' from ideas put forward by listeners of Ray D'Arcy's Today FM show. With the Irish team flexing their vocal chords for the song, we soccer fans have also had the chance to sing along via a phone application. All those who took part have had their voices added to the song. The Dubliners, The Coronas and Bressie alongside Damien Dempsey are contributing to the single and proceeds from sales of the single are going to the Irish Cancer Society's Shave or Dye campaign and the John Giles Foundation. And get practising because it's a tough one to sing, even after five pint bottles of cider.

The Rocky Road to Poland

T'was in the merry month of June from our home we
    started
Left old Eireann's isle, to Poland we departed
Hope within our hearts.
We can win a trophy
We're a part of Trapattoni's army,
Get behind the team, hear the Irish scream,
C'mon you boys in green, Ireland's bouncing back
    again,
We have got our Trap, the cat is in the sack,
We'll not forget you Jack on the Rocky Road to
Poland.
One, two, three, four, five
Irish eyes are smiling
Let your voices ring,

Trapattoni's army,
Everybody sing
You'll never beat the Irish (x 4)
Make your mother proud, inflate your plastic
    hammer,
Bate your bodhran loud and learn your Polish
    grammar.
Credit union loan, sold the Opel Corsa,
Hired a camper van, picked it up in Warsaw,
Been so close before, hopes slammed in the door,
Now we're back for more, we can win the battle,
C'mon you boys in green, never have we seen,
Such a fearless team on the Rocky Road to Poland.
One, two, three, four, five
Irish eyes are smiling
Let your voices ring,
Trapattoni's army,
Everybody sing
You'll never beat the Irish (x 4)
Ireland abú. We love.

Acknowledgements

Thanks to the various bottles of beer that kept me awake until 3.00 a.m. so I could finish this book. Thanks to my wife Dorota and daughter Mia for putting up with tripping over these bottles that covered the floor of our apartment for about four months. Thanks to Elizabeth, Nuala, Ailbhe and Benil and all at Orpen Press for their great work.

A special thanks to freelance sports journalist Jonathan O'Meara for encouragement, tips and proofing. Thanks also to Dr Harry Browne of DIT, John Barrington of nineteen21 Photography, and YBIG's Liam Murray, Enda Corcoran and Eoghan Rice for their help. I am grateful to Eddie Brannigan at the Irish embassy in Warsaw and Wojciech Częgiel at the Polish consulate in Dublin for their help and encouragement.

Oh yeah, and I nearly forgot you Gerald Hough, my doppelgänger. A maestro of all things Polish, Gerald was a key man to consult regarding chatting up the locals, avoiding serious punch-ups and living on less than 1 zloty a week, and to share views with on what makes Poland a great destination for Irish people. And to leave the best wine until last (even though they are teetotallers), a very special thanks to my brilliant mum and dad who brought me up to love sport as much as I love them.

I hope you all enjoy reading this book as much as I did writing it.

Contents

Contents

Contents

1. Introduction

Close your eyes, take a big slug of a pint, dream.

We beat Croatia in a 2–1 dream start. Roughing up Spain, we concede early in the second half before Robbie scores a beauty for a 1–1 draw. Next, we score an early goal against Italy and defend like warriors to hold out. We're second place in the group, topping Italy by goal difference.

Next up, France in the quarter-final. Aaah, France – revenge, sweet revenge. Duff does an 'Henry' and handles the ball before scoring. This victory tastes so sweet. Swivel on it, Thierry!

A semi-final fixture pitched against the almighty Germans. We go down 1–0 early on to a Klose header. Germany get a man sent off, and then Robbie steps up and we pot a penalty equaliser with 20 minutes to go. Extra time, we defend desperately. Penalties! Will it be Spain 2002 all over again? The Germans are clear favourites, but Given saves two and they hit the post … it's wide! Richard 'The Iron Curtain' Dunne steps up to the penalty spot … it hits the inside of the post – a goal! We go through to our first ever Euro championships final. Against? The Netherlands.

We're the underdogs, but as we know from Euro 2004, in the final, everything is possible.

Eight years ago, Greece were ranked no. 35 by FIFA when they captured the Euro 2004 title. Ireland's current FIFA ranking is at no. 19, so at least on that front we can be justifiably hopeful.

Sure, we've drawn the death penalty group, but maybe you are old enough to remember Jackie's army, the surprises and joy they gave us. Who's to say Trap's army won't continue their streak of luck in June. Our infamously negative football pundits? Let's remember what Brendan Behan said: 'F@#k the begrudgers.' Let us bask in the glory of our qualification. Euro 2012 is going to be a moment to treasure. And who knows when we'll qualify for another championship!

As you probably know and have experienced while travelling abroad, getting ripped off sometimes goes with the territory. If you are already on a tight budget, and your Euro is even worth anything in seven months' time, this guide will help you plan well, meet fantastic Polish people, cut costs, order a pint in Polish, record game results, refer to key football facts, avoid run-ins with idiots and hooligans (Irish, Polish and others); and maybe even pick up a good-looking Polish partner for yourself.

This guide won't tell you what colour towels different hotels have, where the best strip clubs are, or how to invest in the Polish property market. It will, however, give you lots of handy football info. and useful cultural and sightseeing tips to make your trip as memorable as possible. Also, I hope it will serve as a nice souvenir to have from what is bound to be a trip of a lifetime to this gorgeous, culturally rich country that I have spent the past six years in.

Some fans will be getting up at 5 a.m. the morning after we draw with the European and World Champions Spain to do some sightseeing. As they pose for photos at the famous Solidarity Shipyard in Gdańsk they might meet other fans singing the 'Fields of Athenry', having spent all night at a local house party. I hope this guide gives all types of fans what they need while visiting Poland and maybe Ukraine during Euro 2012 or supporting from home.

And if you see an Irish-looking fella speaking Polish in a pub, then maybe it's me! Watch out for the receding hairline and foul mouth. I've been here since 2006 and am enjoying every bit of it. I got married a year and a half ago and Dorota and I have a beautiful, half-cracked 18-month-old girl, Mia. Oh yeah, and a fully-cracked but hilarious Polish cat who can open the fridge door all by himself.

I recently heard that a third of Polish marriages collapse so I best be careful. Maybe mine will also start to crumble if we make it to the Euro finals, and a few weeks later I'm pulled out of a ditch penniless and 100 miles from home after going AWOL.

Euro 2012 Trivia: The official match ball for UEFA Euro 2012 is the Adidas Tango 12.

2. Recent Irish–Polish Relations

Irish–Polish football trivia:

- Our first international senior soccer team to play Poland in Warsaw was in 1938, just one year before the outbreak of Word War II. We lost 6–1.

- Packie Bonner may not have such fond memories of Poland. He made his debut in Bydgoszcz 31 years ago, letting in three goals. The first came after just 90 seconds and later on Dave O'Leary scored an own goal.

- It has been 36 years since the first and only time we won a game in Poland. We defeated the home side with Don Givens scoring twice.

- One year after the football mania of Italia '90, we met Poland for the first time competitively in the Euro qualifiers. A goalless draw in Dublin preceded a 3–3 draw in Poznań. Paul McGrath, Andy Townsend and Tony Cascarino hit the mark for us, but we conceded two late goals. Let's hope history doesn't repeat itself. (Source: FAI Official Programme, 19 November 2008)

Commentators frequently talk about how Polish and Irish people are alike. That we're Catholic, suffered hardship under our neighbours, love spuds, worship alcohol and have a national pastime of emigrating and complaining. That we are great craic, amazing hosts, passionate and entrepreneurial. That's all fair enough; it helps break the ice and is a large part of the reason why we get on so well.

Spend a little time here though and you'll soon get to see just how truly different we are. Different, that is, in many wonderful ways that makes us find out something new about each other every day. There's never a dull moment in Irish–Polish relations, but we tend to always be even closer despite the struggles we sometimes face in communicating and understanding each other better.

Let's go through a few of these sticking points.

i. Key differences

First and foremost, they start drinking and socialise mainly in each others' homes – while we tend to start drinking in parks and spend half our lives in pubs.

They go to church every Sunday, whereas we now often only go if it's followed by a session. Their priests and nuns wear religious clothes in public – shock, horror – and nobody spits on them or crosses the road with their kids. The church here hold a lot of sway; the church in Ireland seems to have had its day. Despite this, we are both still very culturally influenced by Christianity.

Most Poles live in apartments; only 4 per cent of us do. Poland is nowadays very mono-cultural – officially, just 0.1 per cent of the entire population are foreigners. Ireland is the complete opposite, our population being made up of 11 per cent foreign citizens. A century ago Poland was a haven for tolerance of peoples from various backgrounds.

They don't wear silly uniforms to school – we do. They think about what they wear – we generally don't. They have four different seasons – we have one. They drink vodka straight. Yes, they drink vodka – straight! We poison it with orange juice or cola.

They find it hard to get visas to the US – we often breeze in. They can speak their own language – most of us shiver when he hear Irish. They experienced Nazism and Communism. We experienced the British Empire and the Vatican. They've got Chopin and Marie Curie – we've got Bono and abysmal A&Es. Ok, we've also got Joyce and James Reilly. They control their own finances – the troika controls ours.

Since they joined the EU in 2004, we've all come to know Poles in our workplaces and social circles. Maybe they work with you or made you feel pathetic when they flexed their huge biceps in the gym. Maybe the Top Model curves of Polish ladies intimidated you.

Maybe you envied your skinny blonde co-worker as she munched down a Supermacs snackbox at lunch, but you knew you had to go with the dreaded salad option. Maybe you heard the surname Kowalski was playing corner forward or at centre-half on your kid's local GAA or soccer team.

Maybe they have been a tenant in your second house. Served you a rasher sandwich or roll in Spar. Checked out your shopping in Aldi and Supervalu.

Fixed your teeth, car, boiler, computer or taken care of your kids. Maybe they were your supervisor or boss? Wherever you have encountered them, over the past eight years, one thing is for sure – it has been hard to avoid them. And, as I'm sure we'd all agree, who'd want to, as they're as nice as you can get.

March in support of the Solidarity Trade Union in Dublin, organised by the Irish Polish Society.
Credit: www.irishpolishsociety.ie

You might be surprised to hear though that Poles have been very active in Irish society much earlier than 2004. According to Patrick Quigley, the Irish Polish Society (IPS) was set up in 1979 just before Pope John Paul II visited. Officially, there were only 150 Poles in Ireland at the time.

When the Polish Communist Government, under General Jaruzelski, declared martial law in 1981 to fight growing support for the free Solidarity Trade Union, thousands were interned and suppressed while basic supplies were either not available or rationed. In the following years the IPS organised concerts, collections and led vigils.

An All-Priests Show was put on in the Olympia and a charity gig in Dolly Heffernans to muster up cash for the Polish Relief Fund. A member of the IPS, Jan Kaminski, demanded RTE broadcast the terrible conditions Poles were having to endure.

During this crisis period in the early 1980s, the IPS sent twenty containers and £250,000 worth of supplies to Poland, including medicine, powdered milk, baby food and clothes. They were brought free of charge, leaving Dublin Port by ship and entering the Polish port of Szczecin, west of Gdańsk, where Ireland will play Spain on 14 June. Our solidarity with Solidarity was maybe the modern birthplace of our positive relations, which continue to grow to this day. The IPS remain active and can be located at 20 Fitzwilliam Place in Dublin 2.

While back in Poland...

The current Polish Prime Minister, Donald Tusk, public enemy no. 1 for football hooligans due to his tackling violence in stadiums, had a mantra a few years ago – 'we're going to build a second Ireland in Poland.' It's not something one would like to be reminded of given our economic woes. That said, we did do well for a very long time, and Poles worked very hard in Ireland over the past eight years, being an essential ingredient to our growth, but also saving and sending back home almost €5.5 bn in savings. Many have settled down throughout Ireland and are active members of our community.

Every now and then, though, something crops up to try and throw a spanner in the works and make our relations go sour. A couple of years ago there was media scaremongering of 'No Irish Need Apply' signs on Polish building sites. The Irish embassy in Warsaw investigated and found it baseless.

In fact, the Irish have always been welcomed with open arms in Poland. For good reason too. Estimates vary, but about 500 currently reside in Poland, with planefuls of businessmen and tourists (religious pilgrims, stag parties and mates of Aga or Wojciech) visiting every week.

Even as I write, very recently one major Irish newspaper mistranslated a very in-depth article in the Polish press about 'Magda', a Polish woman who has lived and worked in Ireland for years. It makes her out to be a sponger and creates an impression that Poles are good-for-nothing leeches on the state's coffers, when in fact the original article is completely different. 'Magda', like hundreds of thousands of Irish, is desperately seeking proper training and job opportunities to create a future for herself in Ireland.

Thankfully, such garbage media is the exception rather than the rule, and Polish–Irish relations will continue to prosper when the storm passes.

ii. The Irish in Poland

And there is good reason why it will. The Polish Ministry of the Interior released figures in 2011, which revealed that Irish people have purchased 110,000 square metres in Polish property over the past six years, while Poland is among the top ten global export markets for Irish indigenous exports. For example, I even put Sudocrem on my kid's bottom if she gets nappy rash, while her favourite food is Irish cheddar cheese.

In 2010, the first GAA club opened in Warsaw. For now they only play Gaelic football but they have been taking part in the European GAA championships – both men and women's teams – and have seen good success to date.

The longest running Polish–Irish group, the Irish Culture Foundation, is based in Poznań and was set up in 1992. They have done trojan work over the years in promoting Irish culture. Irish dancing is generally adored here, as is our capacity to drink stout by the keg. But this group have ensured that Poles know we're not only bowzies who love the gargle. Our trad. music and dance are very popular, as are our actors, writers and our ability to punch above our weight in all fields.

Irish firms Sisk & Sons and Roadbridge are helping build part of the A1 motorway that runs south of Torun and includes 94 km of new motorway and 75 km of side roads, as well as six major interchanges, 88 bridge structures, six toll plazas and ten motorway maintenance/service areas. Many Irish workers have been key to the €624 million project and we can take pride in the fact that they are a big part of the reason people will travel safely and quickly through Poland by road for matches, business, tourism, well into the future.

If you've already been to Poland you'll understand the title of Tom Galvin's book *There's an Egg in My Soup*, about his experiences living in the Polish wilderness. When you eat here during the championships, make sure you don't choke on the various foodstuffs they peg into their delicious soups. It's worth having a read of when you get back home from the championships, as it'll give you a fairly unique insight into what daily life was like here almost twenty years ago.

On 26 August 2010 the city of Gdańsk honoured Sean Lester by naming a room in the Town Hall after him. L–R: Paul McNamara (author), Ann Górski (Lester's daughter), Declan O'Donovan (Irish Ambassador) and Bogdan Oleszek (Chairman of Gdańsk City Council). Credit: Bartłomej Borowczak

Irish historian and English teacher Paul McNamara has also recently written a book, *Sean Lester, Poland and The Nazi Takeover of Danzig*, about one of Ireland's hidden treasures, diplomat Sean Lester. As a member of the

League of Nations, he was stationed in the Free City of Danzig (now Gdańsk) from 1937 to 1939, at the same time the Nazi party were seeking to take control of the key coastal city. Lester frustrated their efforts for some time before being expelled from the city in 1939. On 1 September 1939 the Nazis invaded Poland. Lester's brave stance in opposing fascism was rightfully honoured by the city of Gdańsk a couple of years ago.

So all in all, our relations are thriving, and the high possibility of Irish–Polish babies being conceived during the championships this year are bound to further strengthen our ties.

Crooked House (*Krzywy domek 11*) in Sopot. No, you're not drunk already, it actually looks like this. Credit: Jan Bur, Creative Commons, Attribution-ShareAlike 3.0 Unported

3. Travelling to Poznań/Gdańsk

As could be expected, flight seats are like gold dust and many of the key dates and destinations are already booked up. If you don't have your travel plans a few weeks in advance of the opening match, don't fret. Lots of budget options are available. But it's best to plan ahead or you might end up walking or thumbing 1,800 km.

You've probably spent a good few head-wrecking hours on Ryanair's website in search of a €1 flight to Poland. You're gravely disappointed by the price hikes though. En route to the land of Poles, you notice their hot, homepage calendar stewardesses are a little different to your mid-morning fantasies. For two and a half hours they desperately try to sell you stuff (aftershave and toy planes, I mean). You use your haggling skills to maintain the conversation, ordering cans of Bulmers when you run out of things to say. You begin to admire how professional and even more beautiful they look with their clothes on and manage to get their number on a napkin.

Tragically, you wipe your sweaty forehead with it when Poznań's 30 degree heat hits you, and you're left with a smudged mess and a blue forehead.

For direct flights from Ireland to Poznań and Gdańsk, Ryanair and the Hungarian airline Wizzair are undoubtedly your best options. Ryanair go daily but only depart for these destinations from Dublin. Wizzair, however, only go on Wednesdays and Sundays. You'll arrive too late for the opening match with Croatia if you come on Sunday 10 June, as their arrival time on both days is a cruel 1.30 a.m. So, given these limitations and their high cost when added to accommodation and guzzling expenses, let's look at a few other options.

If I were you, I'd be spending the bulk of my time in the Tri-City area of Gdańsk, Gdynia and Sopot. It's on the gorgeous Baltic coast, has many lovely unspoiled beaches and it's a fascinating area for sightseeing, drinking, mating and waking up semi-sober in an unknown doorway at 4 a.m. The weather will probably be piping hot in June so you and your buddies can work on your pale complexion and admire the abundant bikinis or six-packs on view.

Another big advantage to basing yourself there is that both the Irish and German teams will be honing their skills in Gdynia and Gdańsk stadia, so you'll be in good company. The Germans will be staying at Dwor Oliwski Hotel, so keep an eye out for them and have a pen handy if they come running for your autograph.

That's not to say Poznań is not a good spot to set up shop. It has lots to offer in terms of culture and craic and we'll go through this in detail later in the book. Most importantly, remember, when you are travelling between our host cities by train, you'll be going from/to *dworzec główny* (goove-neh) or the central stations. If you are asking for directions or telling the taxi driver where you wanna go, try not get it mixed up with *gówno* (goove-no), which means sh*t.

That's just one of many words that could mean the difference between a long-term relationship with seven children and a black eye, so make sure you browse over the Polish phrases section (Chapter 6) to avoid these cock-ups.

i. Package tours

If you're lazy, lacking time and energy, then consider **the Polish Pass** (www.polishguide2012.pl/en/polish-pass). It's a one-stop shop option for a Euro 2012 package travel offer. It includes accommodation, travel, medical insurance and public transport tickets.

Abbey Travel (www.abbeytravel.ie) are the FAI's official Euro 2012 agent and have day return packages for each game, a two-match package for Spain and Italy, as well as three-match packages.

A morning departure and post-match return for the 10 June game against Croatia costs €599. Match tickets are not included in this. A deposit of €150 per person is required.

Ticket prices range from Category A (€120), Category B (€70) and Category C (€30). You can't buy them directly from the agent, but instead you'll get a password to purchase them online. It's best just to register yourself as early as possible on the UEFA ticket portal (https://ticketing.uefa.com/euro2012-en/default.aspx), the only place where you can get official tickets on resale. The portal closed on 10 April, but the good news is that it will reopen in early May.

Their day trips to the games sold out quite quickly but they may yet be putting more on offer. The Ireland v Spain game, on in Gdańsk on 14 June, costs €579, while the Ireland v Italy game in Poznań on 18 June costs €599. A two-match package to Ireland v Spain and Italy costs €1,899. That includes six nights accommodation and leaves Dublin for Gdańsk at 8 a.m. on 13 June in Gdansk, then departing Poznań after the Italy game.

A three-match package for the games against Croatia in Poznań on 10 June, Spain in Gdańsk on 14 June and Italy in Poznań on 18 June starts from €2,349 per person and includes guaranteed match tickets.

The package includes return flights from Dublin to Poznań, two nights in Poznań, six nights in Gdańsk, transfers (from the airport to the hotel, Poznań–Gdańsk return and stadium to the airport after the Italy game), all taxes, and an Abbey Travel representative. A deposit of €300 is required. You can book these by calling 01 804 7102.

Thomson Sport are the official travel agent partner of UEFA. Their ten-night package includes a return charter flight from Dublin to Poznań, accommodation at the 3-star Novotel Malta Hotel or equivalent in Poznań, access to all licensed match tickets, transfers (including Poznań to Gdańsk for Ireland's match against Spain) and it all costs €2,899 per person. You gotta pay a deposit of €250 and the rest by Spring.

There are also three- and four-night packages to Poznań or Gdańsk for the various games where you'll stay in 3-star hotels. They cost between €1,549–1,699 per person and have similar terms as the ten-day package. You can call them on 01 433 1013.

747 Travel on Aungier Street in Dublin have a long history of bringing fans and expect to bring about a thousand people. Packages are expected to be cheaper, so ten-day packages in 3-star hotels with B&B come to about €1,759-1,995, but you'll also have to battle it out for match tickets.

Bydgoszcz and Torun are their base cities for the three-match packages – good locations between Poznań and Gdańsk and beautiful cities in their own right. They depart Dublin on Saturday 9 June for nine nights and the return flight is from Poznań after the Italy game.

It's a clever choice really, as the games will be ending at 10.45 p.m. local time, and by the time you are out and about it may be 11.30 p.m. Would you really wanna make a five-hour trip to your base city? Not really – so the cities in between the hosts is an attractive proposition. Also, you'll be saving €350-600 compared to Abbey's offer.

Departures on match days will be mid-morn so you'll be able to grab lunch in Poznań or Gdańsk, hit the beach or do some sightseeing around the old towns and chill out around the Fan Zone while doing a few stretches for the big game. Coach transfers are included from the airport, to the stadium, and to the host cities. Call them on 01 478 0099 for more details.

Joe Walsh Tours is looking at contracting hotels on the ground but also doing day trips, similar to what fans were willing to do in previous competitions like Italia '90. Remember, you'll save a bomb by not staying over in Poznań or Gdańsk, so even though the flights will be more expensive you may ultimately save a few bob. They are also offering a free trip, so get registering. Give 'em a buzz at 01 241 0888.

Limerick Travel and **Dawson Travel** in Cork are also running trips so if you're a local then get in touch with them.

ii. Fly and rail

Online flight booking company Skyscanner did research in January to check increases in searches on flights per month to Poland/Ukraine from participating nations. We came out no. 1. Before the December announcement we searched 315 times with them and in December this jumped to 13,627 searches – a whopping 4,226 per cent jump.

With this demand, prices are fluctuating so much it would be pointless to give 'definite' one way or return flight prices here for the various points to which you can access the host cities. But there are still going to be lots of budget options late in the day so don't bite at the first expensive cherry.

Flying and railing is a very good option. German railways are efficient, clean, safe, punctual and well stocked with quality food and drink. Below you'll find proposals on travelling from various European and Polish cities with samples of train timetables. You can find out more details and book online, around three months in advance at www.bahn.com/i/view/GBR/en/index.shtml for international trains or at pkp.pl for Polish trains.

Berlin

An early morning or evening one way flight with Aer Lingus is hovering between €290 on Friday 8 June and €360 on Saturday 9 June. Ten-day returns are €520–600.

The German capital is a three- or five-hour train journey (depending on your departure time) to Poznań. There are three trains daily and it costs about €36 one way for a second class seat. This Euro-City train from Berlin to Warsaw passes through Poznań. You need to reserve a seat to ensure your place. Group discounts for six adults or more are available. You can get well fed and oiled up on board. The 14:40 and 17:40 trains have no transfers so try get on these. They take just half the time of the morning and late evening trains.

For more information or to book your ticket go to www.bahn.com.

There are loads of bus options too and they hover between €30–40 for a single ride ticket and take about three and a half hours (www.berlinexpress.pl, mikrobusy.net.pl, berlintravel.pl). Best craic will be found on the Irish supporter's club 'You Boys in Green' (YBIG) buses. They're running 40 luxury coaches from the Hauptbahnhof in Berlin to Poznań, leaving at 10 a.m. on the Croatia and Italy match days, returning after the games at 2 a.m. They'll even have beer on board at €2.50 for a half litre of beer or you can bring your own drink. It costs around €45 return and you can follow updates on the ybig.ie forum or email casarebelde@gmail.com for more details.

Frankfurt–Poznań

Approximately €112 one way with Aer Lingus or €175 one way with Ryanair. You can take a sleeper train from Frankfurt direct to Poznań. Tickets can and should be reserved three months in advance. Aer Lingus are due to announce a Cork flight to Frankfurt before the games start.

Alternatively, fly to Hamburg for €170 one way with Aer Lingus. Take a train to Berlin and change over for the express train.

London–Hamburg–Gdańsk

Due to the number of changeovers this is probably only for the train geeks or the very adventurous. You start off in London St Pancras, take a three-hour trip to Brussels, change train to get to Cologne, and then change at Hannover and Hamburg before getting on the Gdańsk train. The last leg of your journey would be a mammoth twelve hours but if you take a few tranquilisers or travel with a big group of drinkers and singers you should be grand.

Amsterdam-Poznań

There are five Aer Lingus flights a day from Dublin starting at 6 a.m. and taking under two hours, which cost just €60 one way. Then, you're just a twelve-hour train journey away from Poznań on a comfortable and cheap overnight sleeper train (see train section) or Intercity train. German railways run a service that brings you from Amsterdam airport to Poznań with just one stop over in Berlin.

Or you could stop off in Berlin for a night as you'd arrive in the afternoon.

Taking the train from Amsterdam–Cologne–Berlin–Poznań is an adventure worth considering.

Maybe you smoked too much weed in your house at the weekend and teleported to Amsterdam. Or you decided to spend a couple of days there before the new right-wing government close down the hash cafés.

The 'Jan Kiepura' EuroNight sleeper train (EN447) leaves Amsterdam at 7.01 p.m. and arrives next morning at Poznań at 7.55 a.m. and Warsaw at 10.55 a.m. The costs range from €49 in a sleeper of six, and can increase up to €139 if you want a deluxe room (sleeps one, two, or three) that has a dvd player and tv, hot shower, cctv security. It's a fairly pointless way of spending extra money as you'll be asleep or drinking most of the time and, after all, a train is a train. The fares for the Intercity train also start at €49.

You can also get to Amsterdam with ferries from Harwich, Hull or Newcastle. Buses depart London Liverpool Street at about 7 p.m. and the ferry journey is 11.15 p.m. to 7.45 a.m. You'd arrive in Amsterdam via bus at about 10 a.m. To book online visit www.bahn.com or www.eurostar.com.

Vilnius – Poland: Only for the hardcore

When I first heard that fans were making the trip to Vilnius, Lithuania and then taking a bus to Poznań or Gdańsk, I thought they were absolutely mental. They are determined to make their roundtrip for under €500 and you can contact them at euro2012bus@gmail.com. However, you could be keeping to a low budget with less hardship if you went the Amsterdam Jan Kiepura train route.

That said, the Lithuanian route is a viable option. Take the three-hour Ryanair evening flight into the Lithuanian capital for just €90 from Dublin. Aer Lingus is a little more expensive. If you don't mind actually meeting locals, then stay the night in a cheap hostel. AirBaltic flights to Warsaw depart in the morning, take just three hours and cost €85. There's also a promotional €3 price / standard €14, eight-hour bus to Warsaw from Vilnius with Simple Express departing at 10 p.m. Eurolines Baltic (www.eurolines.lt/) have a number of cheap options too. For trains check out www.seat61.com.

Polish cities – Poznań/Gdańsk

Polish Rail Service are coming out in April with details of extra services during Euro 2012, so if you're travelling to other Polish cities, you can try to book your train ticket (*bilet*) online at www.intercity.pl. Register for free (you need your passport number) and book your tickets online one month in advance of the planned departure date. You'll save a lot of money as compared to going with any additional coach transfers being organised by your hostel, hotel or fan village. Don't try to save money by going on the regional trains as they are literally a pain in the hole.

Below you'll find information regarding train transfers from all the major cities in Poland to Poznań and Gdańsk Główny (central train stations), including fares. Make sure you are in the train station an hour before departure time, especially if you haven't booked tickets in advance.

Tips: When you check out the most up-to-date train schedules on the general Polish rail website (www.pkp.pl), which has no English version, the columns in the timetables (from left to right) show the following: Place of departure and arrival (*Stacja/przystanek*) – date of departure (*data*) – start and finish time of trip (*czas odjazd/przyjazd*) – duration of journey (*czas podróży*) – number of transfers to be made (*przes*) – train type (*środki komunikacji*).

When you arrive at train and bus stations have a look for the Radio Taxi phones: you'll get a better rate from them compared to the hawks lurking around.

Warsaw

There is just one Aer Lingus flight daily, departing Dublin airport at 7.20 a.m. and arriving in Okęcie airport at 11.15 a.m. Polish time. Grab a taxi to bring you to the central train station (€9 or 40 zł / 11 km away) or buy a one-time ticket (*bilet jednorazowy*) to use any of the public buses outside the arrivals hall to bring you to the Central Train Station (Dworzec Centralny), which is next to the Palace of Culture and Science and Jimmy Bradley's great Irish pub. Staying over in Warsaw would be ideal as it has great nightlife and there is really lots to see. Intercity trains between the two cities take just four hours and leave the main train station in Warsaw (Dworzec Centralny). The Warsaw train goes onward to Germany so it's very regular and reliable. Leaving on the hour every hour, the journey takes between three and four hours depending on the time of departure and amount of transfers. The fast intercity train tickets cost about €18 (80 zl).

Łódz

Via Ryanair, a ten-day return flight is about €370. Going via Stansted you might save about €140. The train from Łodz to Poznań takes four to five hours and costs just €12 (48 zł). Łódz means 'boat' in English, even though there is no major river nor do they have any tradition of a boat or shipbuilding industry. Łódz is also a viable option for cheap accommodation. Check out www.en.uml.lodz.pl for more information.

Szczecin

€200 for a one-way trip with Ryanair, it's a good landing spot if you plan on staying in Gdańsk or the Tri-City area. Either hang around the old town district for a few hours or just go direct to the central train station (in Polish: stats-e-ah goove-nah) and take a five- to seven-hour train, depending on the number of changes, to the Tri-City area. The cost of a one-way ticket is a reasonable €15 (59 zł). Your train departure time, here and in every other Polish city, is key to maintaining your sanity during your time here. So make sure you check out www.pkp.pl and www.intercity.pl in advance as peak hour departure times can save you a few hours of delays and transfers.

Krakow

A beautiful place to start your trip to Poland if you can afford a few days here. Catch Italy, England and the Dutch training once you get in via Ryanair's early afternoon arrival. A twelve-day 8–20 June return is a reasonable €280. You can easily grab a train to Warsaw or Poznań after some sightseeing. The quickest trip to Poznań takes only six hours and costs €24 (93 zł) one way. Remember, you can get grub and liquor on board, chat up tourists, stick your head out the window and enjoy the countryside view. Despite a recent tragic crash where two trains collided on this line, leaving seventeen people dead, train travel remains very safe in Poland.

Wrocław

If you fly in (c. €330 return) to Wrocław (host city for Group A – Poland, Greece, Russia and the Czech Republic) in south-west Poland, you are just a €14 (67 zł) and three-hour journey from Poznań. Capital of the Silesian region of Poland, in 2016 it will be European Capital of Culture. A nice, relaxed city to walk around or spend a night in if you have time on your hands. From the airport you can go straight to Wrocław Glowny train station, hop on the train and bob's your uncle.

Rzeszów

Rzeszów is close to the Ukrainian border and Lviv. Fly one way with Ryanair for €120 or for less than €200 for a return. It's a little far from Poznań, but if you have a couple of days to play with then it's a great option as it's just a few hours from the beautiful city of Krakow. Regular trains will bring you from Krakow to

Warsaw in less than three hours. It's another three and a half-hour train journey to Poznań. Or you could just go direct in about ten hours, sleeping overnight and saving dosh on accommodation. Ryanair arrives in the evening but there are still lots of trains to choose from. To ease your pain try to get one that has no, or just one, transfer. The train to Poznań costs about €25.

Katowice

€120 one way or €240 return with Ryanair. The flight arrives in time for you to take a six-hour night train to Poznań departing Katowice at 0.40 a.m – another way to save on accommodation. For the less hardy and those who have a little time to play with, it would be best to make it to Krakow, stay over and then make your way onward to Poznań for the Croatia game. The train is €19 (56 zł) one way and there are hourly options to choose from.

Toruń

This beautiful Polish city unfortunately does not have an international airport so you'll have to arrive at Berlin or Bydgoszcz (Ignacy Jan Paderewski airport) for the best budget options. The train from Poznań to Torun takes just two and a half hours and costs €10. From the station you can take the no. 22, 25 or 27 bus to the city centre. A ticket costs €0.60 (2.50 zł). You can buy it in any shop or on the bus (exact change required). A taxi costs about €3.50–4.80 (15–20zł). Since early December people have been organising bus travel on the Irish Supporter's Club portal (ybig.ie). There are still lots of places, so contact euro2012bus@gmail.com if you are interested. Greenforever and Steve Krijger have sourced local buses making trips to Krakow/Auschwitz/Wieliczka saltmines. It costs €20 for a return trip to Poznań or Gdańsk. It costs €20 for a day trip to and from Warsaw for games there and €40 for trips down as far as Krakow.

Bydgoszcz

Ryanair are cashing in on the fact that this city is located between our two host venues. Return flights around the group games cost €500. Aerlingus don't fly here. If you base yourself here it's probably due to cheaper accommodation options. You'll probably be coming in from Berlin. Keep an eye on budget options from Stansted too. Trains from Poznań take two hours and cost less than a tenner. The service is very regular as it also serves Gdańsk and the Tri-City area.

iii. Driving to/in Poland

Don't forget to bring a 'flahsk of tay' and a 'hang-sangwidge'.

First of all, you're not seeing things boggly! Poles do drive on the right-hand side.

When Joxer went to Stuttgart he met the woman of his dreams. 24 years later, his twin son and daughter, lovingly conceived at the back of an Irish pub after the England game, are as barking mad as he was in his prime.

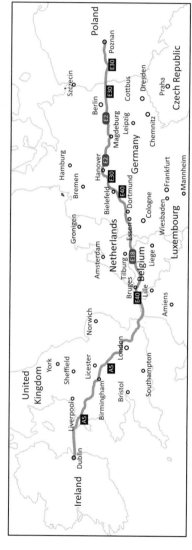

Map 1: Dublin to Poznań route – only 1,900 km, or 1,650 km if you're a bird.

Here are **ten key things** Joxer, his missus and their kids should remember to get to Poznań and Gdańsk safely:

1. Dipped headlights are obligatory at all times while driving in Poland.

2. Warning triangles must be used during an emergency.

3. Let your credit/laser card issuer know you will be travelling abroad so you don't find yourself with a suspended card at a filling/toll station if they spot it being used in unfamiliar places. Petrol and diesel prices are at an all-time high here, and may climb to €1.30 (6 zł) per litre by June.

4. Third-party insurance is compulsory. A green card is advisable and your insurer should be advised of your trip.

5. Obey speed/alcohol limits: Motorway – 140 km/h; dual carriageway – 100/120 km/h (expressway/ non-expressway); open road – 90 km/h; town/ city – 50 km/h (60 km/h from 11 p.m.–5 a.m.); residential/home zone – 20 km/h; alcohol limit – 0.5 mg/ml (below 0.2 per cent).

6. On-the-spot fines for speeding and traffic offences can reach up to 300 Polish squid (€70). You're entitled to an official receipt, which may put off corrupt cops.

7. When approaching a roundabout give way to traffic already on it and on your left-hand side.

8. Take super-duper-extra care when overtaking. Double overtaking is a national pastime in Poland. Remember, if you say super-duper (*dupa* is the Polish word for 'rear end') Poles will take you are saying they have a fine ass.

9. Bring a service pack of oil, coolant, etc. Make sure you know how to change a wheel, etc. Remember it's illegal to service a car/camper on the side of a major road in Germany.

10. Your foreign number plates will be very attractive to the eyes of the unwanted so park wisely and keep doors locked when stationary. Theft, even of wheels, is an issue you should be aware of and take necessary precautions against.

There are a few cheaper places to buy petrol or diesel in Gdańsk and Poznań. If you happen to be in their general area, you might as well profit from it. In April 2012 the price was around €1–1.20 (4.50–5.50 zł) per litre.

Poznań:
Carrefour – Wojciechowskiego 7/17
Poznań Neste – Zamenhofa/Near Lidl
Poznań Neste – Mieszka I/Next to the central shopping mall
Auchan Tarnowo Podgórne: Św. Antoniego/Swadzim
Intermarche Umultowska 32
Gdynia:
Lukoil/Jet – Wielkopolska 260
Orlen – Wielkopolska 239
Gdańsk:
Lukoil/Jet – Słowackiego 134/C.H. Matarnia, Ikea

ZKM/Hallera 142
Lotos Optima – Astronomów 20 Street – beside 'SELGROS'

If you want to **rent a car** in Poznań, Gdańsk or any other Polish airport, an eight-day rental around the group match dates will set you back around €250–450. There are lots of options (Hertz, Avis, Sizt, Global Car, Europ Car, Budget). You can book them at airport-poznan.com.pl and Gdańskairportcarhire.com.

Legions of us are reportedly snapping up and booking campervans in Ireland and throughout Europe to travel either part or all of their journey to and inside Poland. It has been reported by the Irish press and representatives from private automobile hire companies that demand has been overwhelming and some private campervan owners are cashing in by leasing them to Irish fans for a couple of weeks.

Making the journey from Ireland is a bit of a marathon but bound to be great craic too. A fourteen-day four- to six-berth rental from Celtic Campervans (www.celticcampervans.com) in Dublin from 7–21 June 2012 would set you back almost €1,900. Additional driver insurance is €10 per day, and it costs an extra €10 per day for insurance if you drive in Britain.

You can also rent campervans in Poland: see www.finserv.com.pl; www.kampery24.pl; www.campery.pl; www.wypozyczalnia-kamperow.pl. Alternatively you may be able to source one on boards.ie or polish-forums.com. There's also word of mouth – any Pole you meet, just ask them whether they know anyone back home who has a camper hanging around their back garden. Ask and you shall receive, knock and the door shall be opened unto you. Be brazen – and you never know what might turn up.

Campervan rental costs have been inflated a lot for the Euros, so expect to pay at least 1,000 zł with tax per day (about €230), a service fee of 300 zł (about €70) with a deposit of €800–1,250.

Most importantly, remember Poland has the worst road safety record in Europe and 2011 saw tragically high fatalities. And yet they seem to have far stricter rules in terms of granting driving licences. Everybody has to do 30 hours theory lessons and 30 hours driving practice in a registered school. Many fail the test five or six times before they are allowed to pass.

I'm going to scare the bejaysus out of you now with some figures. In 2011, 4,142 people died in road-related accidents on Polish roads. That's a 6 per cent increase on the previous year. This is in stark contrast to Ireland – we had just 185 killed on the roads in the same period, the lowest number of fatalities since records began half a century ago. Even taking into account our population difference, the Polish road fatality and accident rate is about three times that in Ireland.

Poznań and Gdańsk have many one way streets and the main market square is closed to traffic. Parking is mainly paid – chip cards (only available from the SPP office, the official parking authority) or coins. You'll need to have small change handy. Prices are displayed on the parking ticket machine and the price depends on what area you park in. It's advisable to leave your car at your accommodation and use public transport while in the city. Otherwise, use 24-hour guarded parking areas (usually marked with a giant 'P', adjacent to main roads, surrounded by mesh wire).

For paying parking and local transport tickets you can also download Mobilet for free. It's really simple – open the application, press the 'bus' sign for public transport or the 'P' to pay for parking. You then choose (*wybierz*) and get a ticket (*skasuj bilet*). Next choose how much time you want to travel or park for and then keep the confirmation to show a ticket inspector.

Park and ride car parks will be available at major approach roads to all the host cities, so you can drop off the car and go directly to the city centre, stadium or Fan Zone. Public transport and special shuttle buses will deal with transfers to and from the car park.

There are some new toll roads that you will encounter, e.g. the A1 and A2 motorways. You can pay by all standard debit and credit cards, as well as in Euros (you'll get change in złoty).

If you always failed geography exams at school but have been given the responsibility for booking your group of mates on a flight, don't forget that the city of Frankfurt is in the west of Germany, as opposed to the town of Oder Frankfurt, which is on the German–Polish border and very near Poznań. A guy I know didn't do his homework well, thought he booked a return flight to 'Frankfurt' on the border, but in fact he and his mates are going to arrive and depart 650 km away from Poznań. Enjoy your twelve-hour train journey to and from Poznań, lads!

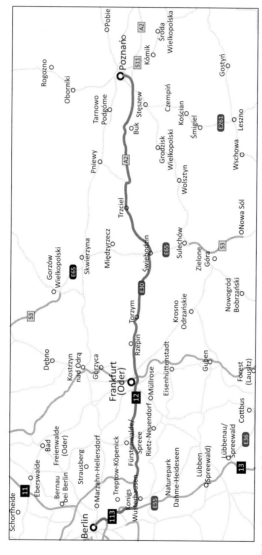

Map 2: Route of the A2 motorway.

A2 motorway (Berlin–Poznań)

Your route from the German border point of Oder Frankfurt should be plain sailing all the way on the A2 to Poznań (see Map 2). It's only about 120 km away.

Coming from Frankfurt (Oder) on the left of the map, the first toll plaza is Tarnawa and here you collect your ticket. Then you will pass by four toll stations (SPOs) at Torzym, Jordanowo, Trzciel, Nowy Tomyśl before paying €3 (13 zł) for a car or €6.50 (27 zł) for a camper at the Gołuski toll plaza (PPO), which is near Poznań. From Frankfurt Oder to Poznań there are filling stations at Gliniec, Chociszewo, Sędięko and on the way back at Zalesie, Rozgoziniec, Sosna. To enter Poznań city branch off at the Komorniki junction onto Głogowska street which will take you bang smack into the heart of the city. If you're religious or bored don't forget to pass through the town of Świebodzin, infamous for its recent unveiling of a Rio de Janeiro style Jesus Christ statue, the world's biggest.

A1 motorway (driving from Poznań–Gdańsk/Gdańsk–Poznań)

The two host cities are 181 miles/291 km apart and you'll have to pay about €4.50 (17.60 zł) for a car or camper. The A1 motorway tolling system is 'closed', meaning payment is made at the end of the journey, at the exit gates. The toll amount depends on the function of the vehicle category and the distance driven on the motorway. Toll stations, except for the main toll plazas in the main corridor, are located on the entry and exit roads (the so-called slip roads) of the motorway junctions.

There are ten toll collection sites along the motorway altogether: PPO Rusocin (Gdańsk–Poznań entrance) and SPO Nowe Marzy (Poznań–Gdańsk entrance) are the ones you need to remember.

When you get on the motorway, collect a single-ride ticket, which allows you to drive any part of the road between Rusocin and Nowa Wieś. You must keep the ticket, as it will be used to charge the toll at the end of your journey.

You'll be passing through the city of Bydgoszcz, which is worth spending a couple of hours in, if not overnight.

There are lots of free applications that can be downloaded and used on your phone to help you navigate your various journeys. JakDoJade.pl (How to go to...) is great for planning your movements around and between cities.

You could also get the freebies Yanosik.pl and Korkowo.pl. These need GPS to operate but will help you avoid traffic and plan detailed routes, identify where cops are with their radar guns, and find out about accidents that have occurred on the road ahead or any blackspots. If you use these applications you will need to know the following words: *miasto* (city), *ulica* (street), *do* (to), *od* (from), *wypadek* (accident).

In Poznań, there are several breakdown service companies available, including: Auto-Bart: +48 515 23 63 62; Kucz: +48 603 09 63 30; Polhol: +48 601 44 49 50.

In Gdańsk, there are REDA: +48 513 81 34 46; HolService: ul. Michałowskiego 41/25, +48 502 66 88 55.

iv. Ireland–Poland by bus

I've done this journey with Eurolines (Eurolines.ie) and can suggest you need a few key ingredients. One may be a well-muscled bum, as the bus–ferry–rail–bus journey takes about 39 hours. Not to worry though, there are pitstops every few hours. I don't regard myself as having a well-toned posterior, and yet found the trip quite comfortable.

Eurolines leave Dublin Busaras every evening at 8 p.m. and arrive in Poznań at 11 a.m. The cost is around €140 single, €200 return. It's more for the experience than anything. You won't see much of Europe though, apart from highways, other vehicles, filling stations and bus terminals. In the past, once you got into Poland, time seemed to stand still for a while as the roads were not as they were in the west; but thankfully the A2 motorway has changed that scenario for your journey into Poznań. Alternatively, if you've only booked a one-way ticket, this might be a good option for coming home.

v. Inter-railing

Inter-railing could be a good way to spend the summer, dipping into Poland for a week to see Ireland's best XI beat the bejaysus out of all who cross their path. If you want an **InterRail Country Pass** for Poland, the table below shows you is what you'll have to fork out for USIT.ie to get it for you.

Duration	Youth (under 26)	Adult (over 26)	1st Class
3 days in 1 month (Flexi)	€51	€77	€118
4 days in 1 month (Flexi)	€62	€95	€146
6 days in 1 month(Flexi)	€83	€127	€195
8 days in 1 month (Flexi)	€97	€149	€228

Source: www.usit.ie

If you get an **InterRail Global Pass** you can't use it in Ireland but can buy a return ticket at a reduced fare (around 25 per cent) from your departure train station to either Dublin city centre, Dun Laoghaire, Rosslare, Shannon, Cork or Belfast (i.e. your point of final departure from Ireland). Even though the Schengen agreement has tightened up over the past few years, you'll travel with ease unless you are a drug mule, human trafficker, make a dumb Nazi joke to the nasty-looking German border police, or stare too long at the Polish border policewoman's breasts.

InterRail Global Passes are valid in 30 countries (unfortunately excluding the Ukraine). There are five options available to you.

Price Level	Youth (under 26)	Adult (over 26)	1st Class
5 days within 10 days (Flexi)	€175	€267	€409
10 days within 22 days (Flexi)	€257	€381	€583
15 days	€298	€422	€6469
22 days continuous	€329	€494	€756
1 month continuous	€422	€638	€977

Source: www.usit.ie

4. Republic of Ireland's Host Cities: Poznań and Gdańsk

i. Poznań

Poznań is in the Wielkopolska province in mid-west Poland, and although it has a similar population to Dublin City with over half a million people, it's well over twice the size of our capital city. The city motto is a cheesy, 'Poznań. Eastern energy, Western style.'

The word Poznań means 'one who's recognised'. It's Poland's fifth largest city and has its roots in a ninth-century island fort on the River Warta. From the end of the 18th century it was under Prussian/German rule. After World War I it was returned to Poland. It was also the birthplace of the first mass protest in Poland against the Soviet bloc.

It has plenty to offer for visitors, so make sure you don't spend all day in your tent, hostel or hotel with a hangover or sleeping on a bar counter.

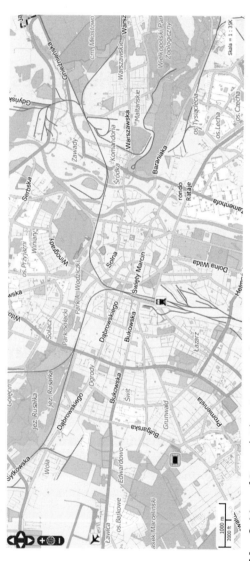

Map 3: Map of Poznań. The airport, main train station and stadium are clearly marked. Between Święty Marcin and Solna you'll find the Fan Zone and Stary Rynek (Old Market). There is a 'second' Stare Miasto (Old Town) next to the Citadel, which is located north of Solna, at Park A. Wodzicki. To the east, over the river, Lake Malta plays host to Camping Malta and the Irish Fan Village just off Warsawska Street. The Carlsberg Fan Camp is just east of the National Stadium in Kasprowicz Park and Łazarz. Credit: www.poznan.pl

Aerial view of Poznań's city centre and the Old Town, Credit: Monika Mężyńska, Creative Commons, Attribution-ShareAlike 2.5 Generic Licence

ii. Ten things to do in Poznań

1. Visit a milk bar (*Bar Mleczny*) – Remnants of communist times, these cheap restaurants remain popular among students and people on a shoestring budget. You'll get well fed on traditional Polish food and although it may not be the best place to bring your new Polish girlfriend on a date, it'll certainly save you some serious beer tokens, the food is solid and you'll meet some ordinary locals. Most of them won't have menus in English so have a look at Chapter 8 of this book to know what's on offer. Also see 'Tip: Don't forget to eat in a milk bar' in the Gdańsk section of this chapter for a sample menu. You can find milk bars on ul. (street) Dąbrowskiego 39, ul. Szkolna 4, Nowe Miasto (New Town), Piastowskie, os. 69, Plac Wolności. So keep your eyes peeled for Bar Mleczny shop fronts.

2. Play pub golf – The best news you are likely to hear is that pubs don't have to close at night in Poland. I'd say it again but you're already uncontrollably leaping up and down with excitement. Poznań has some lovely spots to cool down from the city heat. You might want to leave some Irish pubs for the final holes on your pub golf. The Dubliner is on ul. Al. Niepodległości 8/82. O'Morgans Irish Pub is on ul. Wielka 7 – it would be rude not to call in. Charymza near the city centre on Slusarska 6 St. is a place worth popping into, while Alter Ego in the Old Town Market (no. 63) boasts the longest bar in the city.

3. Explore Poznań with a City Card (*Karta Miejski* pronounced Karta Meayski) – Available for one (€7 or 30 zł), two (€9 or 40 zł) or three days (€10 45 zł), it offers free use of public transport, free admission to most of Poznań's museums, discounts in sporting and recreation venues, various hotels and restaurants. Buy it at the tourist information centre, Old Market Square

Poznań City Card. Credit: www.poznan.pl

Map 4: Map of the Old Market Square: Credit: www.poznan.pl

or in hotels. It gives you discounts at interesting places like the Museum of Musical Instruments, the Lech Visitors Centre, New and Old Zoos, Maltanka Miniature Railway and at Malta Ski you can save a few złoty on the summer sled track, play mini golf or go downhill rafting. Make sure you sign your name and the date on the card and have your passport or drivers licence with you or it'll be treated as invalid.

4. Hangout in the Stary Rynek (Old Market Square – see Map 4) – Located near Wodna Street, it's chilled out, beautiful and full of cafes where you can try *Sznek z glancem* (sweet rolls with sugar icing) and St Marcin's croissants. Drink a beer outside–while admiring the sights of course. The Stary Rynek has as its centre point the Town Hall (*Ratusz*), one of many architectural gems. It's the heart of Poznań and the place where you will best see what Poznań has to offer. Pick up some souvenirs of Poznań's billy-goats (*Bamberka*) and 'pyry' after we beat Croatia and Italy. The Old Market is close to the Fan Zone and the fan camps and is also a treat for any visitor.

You'll be near the Town Hall, home to the Historical Museum of Poznań and a few very odd-looking clocks. When it strikes midday, watch out as two metal goats appear from small doors and butt horns twelve times. It's believed that during the clock's original unveiling, two goats escaped and started fighting above it. Therefore they were immortalised through this interesting display.

5. Play golf – For those of you warned by your missus not to swing on the dancefloor, you can instead swing all you want at the golf club in Bytkowo, County

Poznań, ul. Pawłowicka 3b, Bytkowo 62–07,0 Roki-etnica. Green fees cost 100–120 zł. Contact details are as follows: tel./fax: 061 66 50 656, e-mail: biuro@golfclub-bytkowo.pl and website: www.polegolfowe.pl. There is a pitch and putt course at Bachalski Sports Park (ul. Wichrowa) (+48 616 63 85 75/golf@bachalski.pl). Maybe stick pictures of Spanish players on your balls (golf balls, that is) at the driving range on ul. Wiankowa 2 (+48 618 78 22 22). Golf is regarded as a sport for snobs here, so don't worry if you get some odd looks while asking for directions. You can hire clubs and get shoes on site. But do call them before-hand to check everything is ok for your visit.

6. Access free internet in the main market square, Poznań Plaza or Stary Browar. Use wi-fi internet at the City Information Center on Ratajczaka Street, the Castle on St Martin Street, exit to the International Fair, Old Brewery at Polwiejska Street. In this way you can keep tabs on everyone at home, Skype your family and let them see the surroundings, book your flights or organise your trip to Ukraine when we qualify from the group.

7. Ride a cucumber – No, it's not a slang Polish term for a long-legged blonde or hunky guy. This was the nickname given to a Czechoslovakian bus popular in Poland during communist (or PRL) times. You can book a tour of the city on one or else do the Maltanka Park Rail, from Maltanka Station in Śródka to Zwier-zyniec at the New Zoo.

8. Visit the Lech Brewery – You've probably seen Lech beer on your local supermarket shelves. The

Lech Visitors Centre (Wielkopolskie Breweries) is at ul. Szwajcarska 11 and claims to have the most technically advanced brewery in all Europe. It's only €1.20 (5 zł) for a tour. The brewery is normally open to the public from 10 a.m. to 8.30 p.m. on Monday and Wednesday and from 10 a.m. until 2 p.m. the remainder of the week. If you're with a group then try to ring a day or two in advance for a two-hour tour (+48 61 667 74 60) or send an email to swiatlecha@kp.pl. Tours usually take place around 10 a.m., noon, 2 p.m., 4 p.m., 6 p.m. (last entry). Tickets are €2.85 (12 zł) and only adults are allowed. If you're driving there then it's opposite the M1 shopping centre, 10 km from the city centre. By public transport from Środka Station or Baraniaka Street you can go by bus no. 84 – it's only about 25 minutes. They also produce Tyskie, Żubr and Redds if you fancy trying them out later that evening.

9. Chill in the Citadel – nice place just 15 minutes' walk from the Old Town. It used to be a vineyard, then it became home to a colossal fortress under the Prussians. In 1945 it was destroyed but the ruins can still be seen. It's a great place to put by a few hours, play a game of football, recover from the previous night's onslaught and mentally prepare for another challenging night of socialising.

If you are a movie fan or history buff, then you might be interested in knowing that the graves of the soldiers on whom the movie *The Great Escape* was based, rest in peace in the Old Garrison Graveyard. 18,000 Polish, British and Soviet troops died here during World War

II. It's also home to two museums, of weapons and the Poznań army. The Campervan village filled with 'Joxers' and 'Joxeresses' is nearby.

10. Go clubbing – Poznań offers a lively nightlife scene and is at the forefront of electro and dance music in Poland. Top clubs include the following. Alcatraz – in the centre of Poznań – is one of the best nightclubs in the city. Cute can be found in a basement beneath Stary Rynek and has good house music. Rapport is a hip-hop club, Lizard King holds live concerts. SQ is in Stary Browar (the Old Brewery) has open air events like 'Goraczka w miescie' (fever in the city).

Kukabara is a classy club with a stylish bar, dance floor and plenty of seating. They often have themed evenings and top DJs. In other words, you ain't going to get any sleep and probably don't even need accommodation. You could just party all night then go sleep in the Citadel park.

> **Tip:** If at any stage you find yourself in need of a pharmacy then look out for *Apteka* – there are a good few open 24/7, for example Galenica on ul. Strzelecka 2/6, Centralna – ul. 23 Lutego 18 or Winogradzka – os. Przyjaźni 141.

iii. Poznań's stadium

Poznań's Stadion Miejski (see Map 5) can be found at Bułgarska 17 Street and has a capacity of over 43,000. It's the home ground of local football clubs Lech

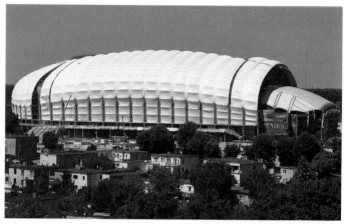

Stadion Miejski (Poznań Stadium), Lech Poznań v Górnik Zabrze, 2008. Named after Lech, the legendary founder of Poland, Lech Poznan have just celebrated their 90th anniversary and affectionately call themselves 'Kolejorz' or 'The Railwayman' due to the ground's location. Their fans are called the Ultras and the stadium cost €160 million to reconstruct. Credit: Ehreii, WikiCommons , Creative Commons, Attribution-ShareAlike 3.0 Unported Licence

and Warta Poznań and its two 116m^2 screens are the largest in Poland. Sting and the London Royal Philharmonic Orchestra played at the official opening two years ago. When you're inside, look up: the roof is a silk-coloured membrane sheathing, lit up by 195 LED projectors which allows it to suit whatever events are taking place at the stadium.

During league matches it is sometimes blue. When the Polish National Team plays it's white and red. Soon, it'll experience a Sea of Green from Trap's army.

A historic bunker stands in one corner of the stadium – part of fortifications from the late 19th, early 20th century. Builders discovered it while carrying out groundworks and it was decided to keep it as part of the stadium environment.

There are 266 places for persons with disabilities in Stands I, III and IV. The Fan Zone at Plac Wolności in the city centre is about 4.8 km away or about 45 minutes by car in high traffic. Beer is available on site, but it'll only have a maximum of 3 per cent alcohol. Stock up before kick off as the stands selling it will be thronged at half time from your thirsty fellow fans.

Getting to the Bułgarska Street Stadium from the centre is no problem. Take the following tram numbers going in these directions: 1 (Junikowo–Zawady); 6 (Budziszyńska–Miłostowo); 13 (Junikowo–Starołęka); 15 (Budziszyńska–(PST)–os. Jan III Sobieski). You can also take bus A, 50, 63 or 91.

If you're driving, you need to get on Grunwaldzka Street, which runs from the centre of Poznań all the way out to the stadium. If you're coming from the Camping Malta site, get on Warszawska Street, head across the river onto Male Garbary and onto Solna. Then, after Stare Miasto take a left onto Kaziemierza Pułaskiego/Franklina Roosevalta. Take a right onto Bukowska and soon after a left onto Grunwaldzka. The stadium will be on your right-hand side. There are 1,600 parking places outside the stadium so get their early.

My advice is to leave all vehicles where you're staying – saves fights over a designated driver when you want to drunkenly celebrate our victories.

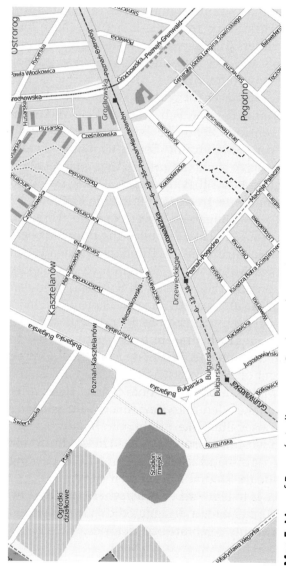

Map 5: Map of Poznań stadium area. Getting to the stadium is a breeze – just follow the yellow brick road. Credit: www.poznan.pl

Beautiful bird's eye view of Gdańsk and the Baltic coastline.
Credit: Leineabstiegsschleuse, WikiCommons, public domain

iv. Gdańsk

Gdańsk is a little bigger than Poznań, located in the province of Pomerania with a population under half a million. The city motto is like an Irish 'drink sensibly' advert – 'Neither rashly nor timidly'. Whoever thinks up of these slogans should really go beyond Google Translate for one-liners.

Napoleon once reportedly said that the 'key to the world lies with Gdańsk', something borne out by a 1,000-year history that has seen this beautiful coastal city pretty much being occupied and under the control of every worldly nation bar the Faroe Islands. It's next to where World War II started at Westerplatte and hosts the famous former Lenin shipyards, which saw electrician Lech Wałęsa and his fellow workers face the might of the USSR, forming the first independent trade union in the former Soviet bloc.

It's the largest part of the Tri-City (also Gdynia and Sopot) and near the amazingly beautiful but unfortunate named Hel Peninsula. Along with Gdynia and the spa town/Trap's squad base of Sopot (the 'trójmiasto'), it covers over 25 km of the Baltic coast.

v. Ten things to do in Gdańsk and the Tri-City area

1. Lenin/Solidarity shipyards – The Roads to Freedom exhibition in the shipyards (ul. Wały Piastowskie 24) is a must see. This is where the first free trade union in the Soviet bloc started. It pays tribute to the Solidarity movement, once 10 million strong though now a pale reflection of its former might, and their fight for a more democratic Poland. You may have seen or heard of Lech Wałęsa over the years. He is idolised outside Poland, but here his legacy as the leader of a revolution is still very much debated. An electrician with a bushy moustache, Watesa, became the first post-Communist Polish president and later Nobel Peace Prize winner, only to fall from grace and power after a couple of years due to Solidarity's turning to a market economy that impoverished thousands of his former supporters. Poland, believe it or not, having had one-third of its population as members of a trade union in the 1980s, currently has one of the lowest levels (15 per cent) of trade union membership in Europe and well below the average (23 per cent).

Stocznia Gdańska (Gdańsk shipyards) in recent years has experienced a lot of financial difficulties. The EU forced the Polish government to stop keeping it afloat with massive subsidies despite huge losses. No political party wants to be at the helm when this historical place sinks. Its gigantic cranes are an interesting sight if you make the Poznań–Gdańsk train trip.

2. Stare Miasto – The Old Town is big and beautiful, fused with lots of character and history and gorgeous surroundings. It is a great place to spend a few hours/ days dining, chatting up other fans, chilling with the family, analysing architecture, bringing someone out for a romantic stroll or binge-drinking. Stroll down ul. Długa and go to a traditional Polish restaurant, taste a Polish-style ice cream, sip on a beer, flirt with the locals or pick up a fridge magnet as part of your souvenir list.

3. Buy and drink amber – You may notice that the Gdańsk stadium is lit up externally in amber. This is because the stone is extracted in large amounts from the Baltic coastline. You'll find lots of nice, locally made souvenirs made from amber so shop around and strike a bargain. In fact, Gdańsk is known as the world capital of amber, so it's really a perfect idea as a gift to purchase some nice local jewellery from the dozens of stalls and shops around.

A local brewery called Amber Browar has won top prizes for both Poland's best pale beer (Żywe), dark beer (Kozlak Amber), and best beer (Kozlak Amber). Make sure you sample them. Also, one of Poland's best-known micro-breweries is at Brovarnia. It's the only mini brewery in the Tri-City and they brew three savage types of beer – Brovarnia Light, Dark and Wheat beer. It's open 1–11 p.m. and is located at 9 Szafarnia Street, Gdańsk.

4. Exercise your calves – If you're a bricklayer, architect, nun or just have a fetish for stairs, St Mary's Church may interest you. Climb its 600+ steps to catch gorgeous views of the city and coastline. It can be found on the beautiful Mariacka Street. It's known as the 'Crown of the City of Gdańsk', and it's the largest brick gothic temple in Poland and Europe. It can hold up to 25,000 people for ceremonies, so if the weather is stormy this summer, city authorities could, in theory, move the big screen into this church so we can watch the games in comfort.

5. Hit Gdynia – Part of the Tri-City and the Irish team's training ground, Gdynia's Sea Towers stick out like the Spire on O'Connell Street. But the seafront restaurants and bars and general chilled-out vibe make it a great place to spend the day. Visit the Donegal pub on Zgoda 10 Street. Ring ahead and tell them to order a few extra kegs 'cause you and your drinking buddies are dehydrated (+48 58 620 46 23/donegal-pub.pl).

6. You may not be into looking at someone's old shoe from a hundred million years ago, but you could chat up a witch at the **Museum of Fables**. It's run by a mythical Kashubian (Kashubia is a region of the area) witch 'Borowa Ciotka' (Queen of the Woods). It's a fairly small museum but, having said that, it's so bizarre it's worth the effort of going.

There are dozens of witches' brooms, folk art, weird dresses. Local legend has it that a witch casting a spell at the same time as you're churning butter could mean a reversal in your misfortune. If Spain go to town on us, ye best get out here quickly (Al. Zwycięstwa

36/108). You gotta ring in advance to arrange a visit so call +48 501 10 21 18 or send an email through her website (www.muzeumbasni.pl).

Or take a gander at the Car Museum. The proprietor started his passion by collecting old motorbikes. He claims he was only eight and did without a few school lunches to save up for them. There are vintage motorcycles, side-cars, a Ford Model T and a classic Mercedes-Benz. Entry is about €1.60 (7 zł). It's open Monday–Saturday 9 a.m.–5 p.m. and is located at ul. Żwirowa 2c (Chylonia) (+48 58 663 87 40/ gdynskie-muzeum-motoryzacji.pl).

7. Is there a bar nearby? That was a regular question I was asked over the past six months when people were asking me about their accommodation choices. There aren't too many places where there isn't. So why not start with a few rounds in the Irish Pub on ul.Korzenna 33/35 or Scruffy O'Brien's pub on ul. Grunwaldzka 76/78, meet up with other fans and have a bit of craic.

If you're sober enough, visit the House of Beer (Degustatornia) whose range of brews are a treat. There are lots of good and cheap pubs and clubs on ul. Do Studzienki (G-4). Other popular places include The Beautiful, Young and Rich, Goldwasser and the Rock Inn Pub. Yesterday serves up some original and pretty strong Polish beer while Klub WieloRyb is a whacky aquarium-looking place. Sfinks seems to operate a good looking only policy so dress up; and Viva is a savage joint altogether.

8. Go to Hel – The Hel Peninsula is a 35 km sand bar, a magnet for kite surfers, sunbathers, jet-skiers, swimmers, banana-boaters, a beautiful nature reserve and a gem for all who love the Baltic sea. It's easily accessible from the Tri-City by train going via the big seaside resort of Władysławowo. The resort of Hel itself has a very cool Oceanography Institute that puts on a seal show every few hours. If there are youngsters in your group they'll especially love it, but I also found it very impressive. The only risk of visiting this place is that you may end up eating a lot of their delicious 'gofries' and pile on the pounds. See Chapter 8 for info. on this Polish delight.

9. Play beach soccer in Sopot – Eat candyfloss on the pier and play beach soccer on the majestic sand. I once saw Damien Duff show off his tricks in Playa del Ingles, so maybe he'll make an appearance outdoors as the team hotel, the Sheraton, is next to the beautiful beaches either side of Brighton Pier, Europe's longest wooden pier at 450 metres. Buy yourself a ball around the area, off with your flip-flops and get dribbling.

Sopot, view from the premier suite of the Sheraton Hotel.
Credit: www.sheraton.pl

Who knows, maybe Trap or an Irish scout will catch you doing an overhead kick.

10. Wanna skinny dip? – Well, best keep your tackle locked up, but head for a swim in the Baltic Sea near Stogi (take tram 3 or 8 to Stogi Plaża (beach)). It is often cold. There are food stalls and bars and lifeguards on duty. Many Irish fans are staying at a well-established campsite nearby so you'll be in good company. The entire 25 kms or so that cover the Tri-City area is a sight to behold and treasure. You can hire out deck-chairs, sun umbrellas, beach cabins or wind shelters. There are are also lots of nice restaurants and bars to keep you well fed and hydrated.

Do you want to find out more about the brave Sean Lester and his work in Poland? Read Paul McNamara's wonderful book on him – *Sean Lester, Poland and The Nazi Takeover of Danzig.* He was from Antrim, the son of a grocer, a Protestant Republican like Wolfe Tone and a member of the Irish Republican Brotherhood (IRB). He helped negotiate peace settlements that ended two wars in South America and this led him to being appointed High Commissioner to the League of Nations controlled Free City of Danzig. So when you're in the Old Town, pop in and have a look at the exhibition for this extraordinary Irishman.

Tip: Don't forget to eat in a milk bar – If you remember to dine on something other than ice cream in between your sunbathing sessions, then these milk bars will save you a packet of money: Syrena on Grunwaldzka 71/73; Neptun on

---

ul.Długa 33/34; Akademicki on ul. Grunwaldzka 35; Perełka on ul. Gałczyńskiego 2; Turystyczyny on the corner of Węglarskiej i Szerokiej; Żuławski on ul. Grunwaldzka 135 (http://smupo.achjoj.info/bary_mleczne:Gdańsk).

A sample menu goes something like this (€1 = 4.20 zł):

Milk (*mleko* 0.52 zł); hot milk with noodles (*mleczna z makaronem* 0.90 zł – it's what kids have in kindergarten); vegetable salad (*jarzynowa* 1.14 zł); pea soup (*grochowa* 1.08 zł); groats/buckwheat (*kasza gryczana* 1.10 zł); young spuds (*ziemniaki młode* 0.80 zł); scrambled egg (*jajecznica* 1.22 zł); custard (*budyń* 0.82 zł); jelly (*kisiel* 0.43 zł); pancakes with sweet white cheese and cream (*naleśniki+twaróg+śmietana* 2.32 zł); white cabbage salad (*surówka biała* 0.75 zł); spinach (*szpinak* 1.11 zł); fried beetroot (*buraczki zasmażane* 0.42 zł); cold beetroot and yoghurt soup (*chłodnik* 1.21 zł). There are lots more to choose from, including Poles favourite '*kotlet schabowy*' or pork chops.

vi. Gdańsk stadium

It took three and a half years to construct at a cost of just under €200 million. Although it has a capacity of 44,000, during the championships it'll be 4,000 less. The stadium's name alone was sold by the city council for €8.5 million for five years. The home stadium of green-wearing Lechia Gdańsk football team, it hosted its first international match in September 2011 between Poland and Germany, which ended 2–2 when Poland conceded a goal three minutes into injury time. Sadly,

PGE Arena Gdańsk stadium is located on Pokoleń Lechii Gdańsk 1 Street. Credit: Dariusz Boczek, WikiCommons, Creative Commons, Attribution-ShareAlike 3.0 Unported Licence

this would have been the first time in their history they had defeated Germany. It's the third largest stadium in the country after the Warsaw and Silesia stadiums.

It's owned by Polish Energy Concern (Polska Grupa Energetyczna), who are also controversially involved in plans to build a nuclear power station in Poland, despite widespread opposition from locals and the country as a whole.

The roof construction is based on 82 girders and has an enormous area of 44,000 m². Four large LED screens with an area of more than 70 m² each are over 6 metres high and 11 metres wide. The interior of the stadium and its surroundings are monitored by 436 cameras (fixed and rotary). There are 2,171 parking spaces for cars and 74 for buses in the area. The facility is also disabled friendly with 50 extra seats.

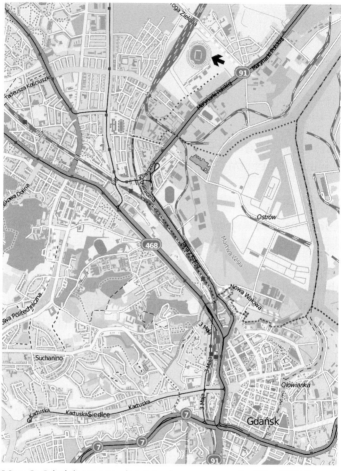

Map 6: Gdańsk-Letnicy district where you can find the PGE Arena Stadium. Credit: © www.OpenStreetMap.org contributors, CC BY-SA 3.0. © www.ump.waw.pl contributors, CC BY-SA 3.0

The stadium's in the Gdańska–Letnicy area near the coast (4.5 km from the city centre – Stare Miasto). Tram

92 or 94 will take you from the main railway station. Go in the direction of Zajezdnia Nowy Port and get off at Załogowa stop or PGE Arena. It takes just 20 minutes. And they leave every 10 minutes.

From Sopot take the the local/regional SKM train to Gdańsk Politechnika station and then change over to tram 92 or 94.

By car, drive north on the E1, which connects Gdańsk city centre with the E7 from Warsaw. The stadium will be unmissable on your left-hand side.

vii. Getting around the host cities

From Poznań airport

Poznań airport is 7 km from the city centre, so as regards the transfer to your hotel or hostel ask beforehand how much it should cost.

Public transport is manageable, comfortable and cheap. When you arrive at Poznań's Ławica airport you can easily get to the city centre by one of these lines:

Line 59: Airport–Bałtyk (Rondo Kaponiera) (30 minutes) or the Express Line L: Airport–Central Railway Station (20 minutes); or Line 48: Wyszeborska (200 m straight from terminal building) – Bałtyk (Rondo Kaponiera) (30 minutes), Night bus line 242: Airport–Central railway station (30 minutes).

From Gdańsk airport

The taxi rank is situated in front of the passenger terminal main entrance. One example of the services offered is City Plus Taxi 9686. The average price is about: €14 or 60 zł (Gdańsk city centre), €17 or 70 zł (Sopot) and €22 or 90 zł (Gdynia).

You can also take a public bus. There is 'B' (from/to the city centre–Orunia) and 110 (from/to Wrzeszcz Railway Station) during the day and N3 (from/to the airport–the city centre or Wrzeszcz) bus line operating at night. If travelling to/from Gdynia, there is a no. 510 bus to/from Gdynia Railway Station. The tickets can be bought from the driver for 2.80 zł (€0.70) – but you need to have the exact change – or from any local kiosk (small stand-alone shops – you'll see them everywhere).

Taxis

Taxis are reliable, in abundance and have meters. Unofficial, dodgier taxi drivers are often hawking around train stations, hotels, popular pubs and clubs and stadiums. Registered taxi services have company name signs on their roof as opposed to a makeshift sign written with tippex declaring 'taxi'. The driver is obliged by law to turn on the meter at the beginning (so check he/she does), to have a cash register in the cab and is obliged to give you a printed receipt for your fare. Consider calling Radio Taxi from the free phones located in the main halls of the various stations you'll arrive at.

There are countless visitors to Poland over the years I've met who get stung by taxi drivers. If you've left it late getting to Gdańsk for the Italy game, get mad drunk on the 13th, sleep in on the morning of the 14th, then you'd be forgiven for forking out half the cost of your house on a taxi ride to make it on time for kick off. Best avoid such scenarios though if you want to avoid a divorce when you get back home.

5-7 zł (€1.25–1.75) is the initial standard charge for using the service, no matter how long or short the journey, and around 2.50 zł (€0.65) or 3.75 zł (€0.95) at night and on holidays per kilometre is the norm. Prices are obviously greater late at night, at the weekend and if you want to go outside the city. Prices should be displayed in the window of the car. So during the Euros, check the displayed prices on the window and you'll be in a better bargaining position if he tries to rip you off.

Always ask at hotel/hostel reception or at your guesthouse the approximate price of the trip you are going to make. I've only ever had good experiences with taxi services in Poland, mainly 'cause I ring ahead and stick with what I know is reliable: I hope you do too. And for emergency purposes, remember that Poznań to Gdańsk would set you back about €270, so it's only to be done if you are flush with cash after winning in a local casino.

Public transport

There are four types of tickets: a) time tickets – valid in buses and trams for the time specified on the ticket; b) single-ride tickets – only valid in buses for the number of stops specified on the ticket (up to ten or more than ten); short-time tickets – 24/48/72 hours or seven days – all services can be used; d) short-time group tickets – 24/48/72 hours, all services for up to five people (only two adults).

In Poznań, the cost for a seven-day ticket for all trams and buses is about €8 (32 zł) and you can buy it in most shops, kiosks and supermarkets. One-time tickets for 15/30/60/120 minutes are also available and cost between €0.50–1.30 (2–6 zł). For one, two or three-day tickets, ask for a normal ticket (*bilet normalny*) and then say (one-day or 'doe-boe-vy' which costs €2.80 (12 zł). A two-day ticket (d-vu-d-nee-o-vy) costs €4 (16 zł) and a three-day ticket (chreh-d-nee-ovy) costs €5 (20 zł). You won't be entitled to any discounts. Trams and buses are frequent and are the best way to make your way around the city.

Don't get caught without a ticket, as fines cost €35 (150 zł). If you are caught, play the dumb tourist. Make sure you always validate your ticket in the yellow machine on the bus, tram or train. If you have a ticket that is not just single use, like a three-day ticket, then you just validate first time round and keep it handy if the inspectors come around.

Register your ticket in the '*kasownik*' (ticket validator machine) or face a hefty fine if you get caught.

Same goes for validating tickets when you travel on the local and regional SKM trains in Gdańsk and the Tri-City area (see Map 7). At the central train station, there are two separate parts, that which deals with long distance, intercity travel and is run by PKP and the SKM-run local trains.

Train transport within the Tri-City is regular and efficient. Gdańsk–Gdynia costs €1.10 (5 zł – 35 minutes). Gdynia–Sopot costs €0.80 (3.40 zł – 15 minutes). If you're soaking up the rays on a bike, bring them to the end of the train. Kids under four need a 0 zł ticket (yes, it's totally dumb). Carry ID with you everywhere and make sure you have a copy of your passport back at your accommodation. If you lose your passport, the embassy or consulate will offer you a temporary document to get home.

ISIC/Euro 26 are useless here. Tickets can be bought at the main train platforms and there is an English-language option so it's easy

Single ticket costs €0.70 (2.80 zł); 60-minute ticket €0.80 (3.40 zł); single fast-line ticket €0.90 (3.80 zł); 60-minute ticket for 'fast' lines €1 (4.20 zł); 24-hour ticket €2.40 (11 zł).

Metropolitan tickets can be used in the Tri-City area for three days. There are two options. One covers buses, trolleybuses and trams. It costs €6.50 (28 zł). The second one includes the local/regional SKM trains (they bring you to Sopot and Gdynia) and costs €9 (40 zł).

Tri-City SKM line. Credit: Leinad, WikiCommons, Creative Commons, Attribution-ShareAlike 3.0 Unported licence

The Gdańsk/Sopot/Gdynia Plus tourist card is also a great option as you get discounts in clubs, museums, restaurants. There are two types: MAX includes free public transport and you can buy a 24-hour card (€10 or 45 zł) or a 72-hour card (€17 or 75 zł). There is also a Standard 24-hour (€5 or 22 zł) or 72-hour (€8 or 35 zł) card that excludes travel. All of these can be purchased at big hotels, tourist information centres, or most city centre shops. Whether you are a tourist or local matters little when it comes to jaywalking – something city cops love to catch you out on. Expect to pay a hefty fine of a couple of hundred złoty.

Map 7: Tri-City SKM line. Credit: Leinad, WikiCommons

The state railway PKP trains are your safest bet when travelling between/outside the host cities. Booking tickets online can be done one month in advance through www.intercity.pl Save yourself some hardship and guarantee your place beforehand. You'll need to print out your ticket and have at hand the document (passport) used for booking. The site has an easily navigable English version.

Of course you can just do it in person when you get here, though queues will be colossal and it'll be hard to come by a ticket seller who speaks English or smiles. Don't take it personally, Poles don't feign being nice. Don't be shy asking someone around to help you (young, nicely dressed, very attractive, no engagement or wedding ring) if you have language problems. They might be only too glad to skip the queue. :-)

The best idea is for you to have your details written down, e.g. *Poproszę bilet* (Please, may I have a ticket): Poznań 08.30 – Gdańsk 12.15 (use the 24-hour clock). After Ireland beat Croatia 2–1, you'll be heading to Gdańsk from Poznań Główny (goove-neh) or central station to Gdańsk Główny.

Poznań–Gdańsk by train

The cost is €22 (87.50 złoty) and you've got quite a few options. To reserve a ticket (*rezerwuj*) or buy a ticket (*Kup bilet przez internet*) go to www.intercity.pl.

Then, click on the English language sign in the top right corner and create an account (you'll need your passport number). This five-minute process is well worth it and will save you being in a queue and maybe not getting a ticket for the train you want.

The Gdańsk–Poznań train is the same cost and lots of extra times are going to be available to choose from during the Euros.

Thousands of Irish fans are expected to travel via Intercity train from Poznań-Gdańsk and back.

Poznań–Gdańsk by plane

Are you 'Siderodromophobic' – in other words, do you have a fear of trains, railroads or train travel? Inter-city plane travel in Poland used to be only for knobs or if you were flush with cash that you could cut your journey to Gdańsk by a couple of hours with a Polish LOT (www.lot.pl) flight. It used to cost about €500 return. But during the Euros, thanks to special flights from Eurolot.com and www.oltexpress.com, it's going to be dead cheap and ticket reservations can be made right now. One-way flights cost between just €25 and €50. So if you plan on maximising your time on the Tri-City beaches, trying your luck with the local talent, then get on board.

5. Recession Accommodation Options

Hotels, hostels, apartments, B&Bs, guesthouses, camp-sites, peoples' back gardens – all may well be booked up or too expensive for you. But don't worry if you haven't planned your accommodation yet and you're pretty much homeless, there are lots of great inexpensive options. And, let's face it, it's nice to experience something different when you are 2,000 km away from home.

Cheap and even free accommodation options are available, let nobody fool you otherwise. If you already have a sleeping bag ready for the back of your car, then you know where I'm headed.

Whether you decide to go couchsurfing, sleep in your car or on the beach, maybe even under a bridge or in the stadium toilets, there are two things to remember – safety and good planning.

Fans are already successfully organising accommodation in local peoples' apartments and houses through Polishforums.com, ybig.ie (You Boys in Green) and boards.ie – great budget options are available if you put out a call. On Facebook there are active pages like 'Irish Fans Travelling to Euro 2012'. Despite a trillion options, people seem to be in panic mode for a roof or tent over their heads. Newspapers in Ireland have put out supplements quoting prices from various 3- and 4-star hotels ranging from €180–380 per night. The good news is that student accommodation has not even come on the market yet.

Couchsurfing.com is not some mad-ass 12-hour binge-drinking game. But it is a great budget option for accommodation during the competition. If you make a one-off donation of €10 you can join a worldwide community of couchsurfers offering a floor, sofa, room or roof of their apartment, house or shed for you to stay in. Younger people from Poznań, Gdańsk and other Polish cities take part in such activities worldwide.

If you intend sleeping rough in your car you'd be well advised to block the windows of the cars with polythene bag, cardboard, newspaper to ensure you don't attract any undue attention from municipal police or louts who are so drunk they think your boot is their bedroom.

Sleeping on the beautiful **Gdańsk beaches** may occur without your prior intention. You could pitch a tent there as the weather will be savage. If you wake up with a seagull eating your shoe then you know it's been a good night. If there is somebody naked beside you, then you may even skip meeting up with your crew and set up camp in the lifeguards hut with your new flame.

Do you have Polish neighbours or workmates at home? Word of mouth may open up basements you would have never thought about. So don't be shy, ask Marcin, Wojtek, Magda and Agnieszka whether their

Sopot has the longest wooden pier in Europe. Its wooden benches make a fine snoozing and candyfloss eating point. Credit: Tomasz Kolowski/Tommy Jnr

great granny has a spare room in their forest cabin outside Poznań or Gdańsk.

In terms of **private apartments** – If you arrive at either city without accommodation then at the train stations and airports there are likely to be accommodation points where you can find out information on how to stay at somebody's apartment for a night or two.

i. Camping in Poznań and Gdańsk

A great way to have an independent trip to and around Poland, hiring a campervan may help you end up saving a lot on accommodation if there are six people splitting the costs. It will also give you the liberty to see hidden treasures around the country. We've dealt with where to hire, now let's deal with where to park them.

You could pitch a tent or park a campervan at Camping Malta, which is located on ul. Krancowa 98. It's 3 miles from the railway station (4.5 km), 2.5 miles from the city centre and 2 miles from the Old Town market. It has a nearby artificial ski slope, tennis courts, bathing beach and bike rental and is located by a beautiful lake.

The campsite has 40 places for caravans, 60 for tents. There are toilets with showers, a kitchen, laundry and tv room. It's a 25-minute drive to the stadium. Call them on +48 61 876 62 03 or +48 61 876 62 02 or email camping@malta.poznan.pl. You can check out their camp here: www.campingmalta.poznan.pl. Another well-known campsite in Poznań is Strzeszynek No. 111. It's located at ul. Koszalińska 15. Tel: +48 61 810 17 00; email: strzeszynek@pooczta.onet.pl; and website: www.strzeszynek.republika.pl.

In Gdańsk Sobieszewo there is Orlinek campsite No. 69 which is located at ul. Lazurowa 5, Sobieszewo Orle. You can contact them on +48 058 308 07 39; email office@harctur.com.pl; and website www.camping.gdansk.pl.

There are a heap of smaller campsites in Poland that exist outside the Euro 2012 period. You can check them out here: http://www.pfcc.eu/ang/main.php?nazwa=start.

ii. Football fan camps

One interesting option is to stay in the Poznań and Gdańsk football fans camp that are going to be available from around 8 June. You'll maximise the craic when you are around like-minded fans and the atmosphere is bound to be brilliant. For prices and to book online check tentresorts.com.

Either bring your own tent (€23 per person per night); or you can be provided a twin tent (two to three people) and it costs €59 per night.

Carlsberg (www.carlsbergfancamp.pl/) are also organising campsites in Poznań and Gdańsk with an accommodation, fan, catering, spot and ECO zones. There'll be 1,500 tents available to rent and the site is well connected to stadiums, the Fan Zone and all city centres. Nearby public transport will help you get between key places. You need to book for a minimum of two days and the provisional prices are as follows:

Single tent (one day) – €45 (190 zł); two-person double tent (per night per person) – € 35 (150 zł); tent equipment (pillow, sleeping bag, foam pad) – €30 (136 zł); lunch – €5.50 (25 zł); parking (per day) – €11 (50 zł).

Within this price you'll get breakfast and two beers – or maybe you can just skip breakfast and have an extra beer instead. The Irish supporter's club, YBIG, were brought over to Poland by Carlsberg in February on a so-called reconnaisance mission. They negotiated a price reduction for fans so it may come to just €25 (112 zł) a head if you stay in a tent or camper. If you want to stay in their 'Dutch House' option, then it'll set you back about €75 per person per night.

The Carlsberg camp in Poznań is located in Kasprowicza Park near the train station and stadium. In Sopot it can be found ner the ERGO Sports Arena and very close to the beach. They are also trying to open another campsite in Poznań.

In terms of booking companies, there are a lot of scam artists. One I know that is genuine and has good deals is Bookingpoland2012.com, run by Tomek Parzybut, a Polish journalist who works with the state broadcaster. I have been helping him communicate with Irish fans as his English is not very good. He's a decent bloke and the boyfriend of one of my students. He got good deals with many hostels and hotels by booking their rooms months before it was announced that Ireland would be playing in Poznań and Gdańsk. He took a gamble and it has paid off. That said, this is by no means the cheapest option you'll lay your hands on. If you're willing to stay in Berlin, Bygoszcz, Łódz or Torun and make the 2–4 hour train journey you'll get a 3-star hotel or nice hostel with twin/triple rooms for about €25 per person per night. So forget all this garbage that you have to spend hundreds of €€€s just for one night. Even UEFA are laughably promoting a budget option that works out at nearly €200 per night. So shop around; follow the Boards.ie, ybig.ie and Thescore.ie accommodation threads online and you're bound to find a reasonable option for yourself and fellow fans.

And if that fails, sure, aren't the pubs going to be open all night anyhow, so why would you need any accommodation in the first place?

One of the biggest let downs for Irish fans holding out for budget accommodation was the collapse of the Irish Fan Village (IFV) in early March. Since then, thankfully, a number of alternatives have popped up, while fans in their thousands are active online every day sharing information about their experiences in contacting different accommodation options.

- **Campervanvillage.com** has given hope to those left abandoned by the IFV. Ironically, and much to the surprise and anger of many fans, it is managed by Łukasz Pawelczak of ABC Events. Pawelczak is already well-known by Irish fans as the face that represented the IFV in the Irish media coverage.

- **Camping Poland** has spaces near the city stadium – more details here: www.campingpoland.eu.

- **Aktywator camp** in Gdańsk is next to the PGE Arena stadium. Their website is www.e-activator.pl. Activator is actually a travel agency, based in Monte Cassino 15/15, Sopot. It acts as the main sales agent for the owner of Activator Camp Rafał Rogacewicz. A tent for two people costs €18 (80 zł) per night so it's a pretty good deal.

If you are worried about your accommodation booking firm or any Polish business you might be transferring money to, then you can check whether they are legitimate here: www.stat.gov.pl/regon. Just find out their NIP (tax ID number) and REGON (business number), enter the details on this website and all their official details should come up. You can also ask them for their KRS (court registry number).

> **Tip:** If you decide to book into a campsite, make sure you bring a big can of mosquito spray with you. The smell of stale beer also tends to help repel them.

6. Polish Drinking Culture

You may be disappointed when you arrive here, as every second building is a church, and not a pub! Poland has about 10,000 pubs at the moment and, funnily enough, almost the same number of churches. Even in my hometown of Banagher we have just two churches and six bars. But don't panic! A recent survey by Zywiec Brewery reckons another 1,000 will open up around the time of the championships. Keep in mind that by drinking lots you'll be helping maintain 208,000 alcohol-related jobs throughout Poland.

Depending on your gut and liver capacity, drinking beer from dusk till dawn may easily supersede all your other costs. If you only drink in your expensive hotel lounge then expect to get screwed. You will be under the illusion that the paper in your pocket is like Zimbabwean dollars, that you'd need to spend cart loads of them in order to make a dent in your bank account at home. But be warned. Many an Irish drinker has come before you, then cried in their pillows at home when they realised they were indebted to their eyeballs.

First of all, you should remember that Poles rarely do rounds. If you are being nice and buy a round, don't expect it to be returned. Equally, don't take it personally if your new Polish friend is adamant he doesn't want you to buy him a drink. I'm still trying to get my head around this and I'm here six years. Shouting them a drink is seen as creating an imbalance in the relationship from the outset, so offer and when you're refused carry on regardless.

They generally do not like it when people flaunt money (avoid leaving your wallet on the bar counter and counting your hundred ztoty notes in public).

Tipping is quite a new phenomenon here but, as always, if you and your group are well taken care of then it's nice to leave the bar man or woman a token of your appreciation. In restaurants it tends to be 10 per cent.

The smoking ban has been in place in Poland since November 2010. Similar to Ireland, you can now smell sweaty armpits of fat dancers and a bit of a beer-fuelled urine pong from the toilets, but the Polish restriction has many loopholes and is certainly less strict than we are used to at home. If you see others smoking, signs with *dla palących* (for smokers) or you can't see but hear people at one end of the pub, then it's safe to light up.

Those of you who have been to a Polish wedding know that they are an orgy of drink, but beer is a rare sight. When I came to live in Poland in 2005 I got the shock of my life when I saw them drinking raw vodka, sometimes 70 per cent proof, then following it by eating a heap of pickles. I started checking flights out the next day. But over time I came to understand that these sour as a lemon, marinated mini cucumbers are a godsend in maintaining one's sobriety. They help you knock back dozens of shots over the course of the evening, without a wobble or puke to be ashamed of.

Think of it as being the equivalent of an Irish person dipping a cucumber into a pint of stout. And having said all that, I suppose at least the Poles are not as bad as the Russians, who only recently decreed beer as being an alcoholic drink.

I have been witness to many a visitor over the years being knocked down due to their inability to stick with their beer. The pressure from Poles to join their toast and skull a 50 ml shot of vodka is relentless, but always in good faith. They will want you to become one of them. But in order to do so, you have to prove your liver's ability for enduring intoxication.

Lightweights are permitted to consume a chaser (*popitka*) after the vodka. Make sure you avail yourself of this. Head for a piss and take a slug out of a bottle of orange on the sly if there are no chasers being offered.

The key to semi-sobriety survival is the age-old maxim – don't mix your drink. Tempters and temptresses will be out to lure you, but remain strong – don't succumb to their attractive good looks or intimidatingly ginormous triceps. When it comes to Poles and drink, my point can be best summed up by recalling a conversation during my own wedding.

One of my wife's uncles, who underwent a triple heart bypass a few years ago, had already knocked back a bottle of vodka by midnight (when you are figuring out how much vodka you need to buy for your wedding here you count a half litre of vodka for every man, woman and child – not a word of a lie). My brother-in-law was trying to get him to drink a beer with him, when the uncle's son ran towards him waving his arms saying 'No beer, no beer, he's sick.'

My bro-in-law laughingly replied in a thick, Mayo accent 'Shur he already drank a gallon of vodka, like.'

To which the son answered, 'The doctor said – vodka isn't a problem, but beer will kill him.'

> **Drinking Tip** – The Dubliner pub in Poznań is located on the corner of Święto Marcin and Niepodległóśći Street and is also very close to Poznań's International Fair market place, where you can find space for camper van parking, electrical hook up, etc. If the weather is a little stormy and it's raining cats and dogs, this is a great spot to keep your head dry and your throat wet.

i. Polish beer

Although Poland plays host to more than 100 breweries, 90 per cent of the market is controlled by just three companies. SAB Miller have the majority stake in 'Kompania Piwowarska', the producers of Tyskie, Lech and Żubr. Grupa Żywiec is majority owned by the Heineken group and make the very popular varieities of Żywiec on the market, as well as Warka, Królewskie, Strong and Tatra, among others. Finally, Carlsberg Polska controls about 15 per cent of the Polish beer market and their main brands include Okocim, Mocne, Kasztelan, Harnas and the top choice of pregnant and breast-feeding women, Karmi (only 0.5 per cent alcohol). Even though Poland is known for its vodka consumption, the range of great quality beers in Poland is very tempting to those who like their liquor. They're the third largest producer of beer in Europe, after Germany and England, brewing 36.9 million hectalitres – that's almost 1 hectalitre of beer for every Polish man, woman and child in the country.

Each Irish person drinks on average 90 litres of beer – draught lager (61 per cent), stout (33 per cent) and ale (6 per cent), and even though in Poland they still drink riverfuls of vodka, they recently overtook us by drinking 91 litres of beer per person. This continues to rise as it's more and more popular among the youth.

We Irish purchase 30 per cent of our beer in shops and off-licences – while the Polish average is around 60 per cent. That's why they have fewer pubs. (Source: Ernst and Young report 'Contribution made by beer to the European economy, 2011'.)

Polish beer is usually quite strong, but in and around the stadium it'll be limited to 3 per cent alcohol level. Cheap pints of Zywiec, Tyskie, Lech and Warka are about €0.75 in a shop (3 zł). Expect to pay three or four times that in a pub. Pay attention to the word *mocne* (strong, meaning 7–8+ per cent) when you are going on a 24-hour session. You can often get non-pasteurised beer on tap and in bottles. Your head will thank you the next day if you choose this option.

Żywe, from the Amber brewery in Gdańsk, is the only Polish beer to have the Slow Food label, and is well worth a sip. If you have any taste buds you'll know the famous Polish brands are also hangover-heavy beers. Do yourself a favour and avoid can or pint number eight and nine. Instead of feeling like someone using a jack-hammer on your brain, you'll wake up fresh as a daisy the next morning and ripe for more craic. There is so much good stuff on the shelves and in the coolers to be only drinking things you can get in your local Tesco or Supervalu down the street. While you're here, try out some of these original, high-quality, reasonably priced delights.

ii. Ten beers every fan (even pioneers) should try

Beer	Review
Okocim Mocne Drunkenly slurred as 'Oh-Ko-Chim Mohtz-neh'	Fast, cheap way to get merry or drunk within two hours. Okocim is owned by Carlsberg. Slugging this back too quickly may transform you into a werewolf, or you may just collapse under a lamppost. €0.80 in a shop. 7 per cent alcohol. ★★★
Żywe Drunkenly slurred as 'Zh-i-weh'	From Gdańsk's famous Amber Brewery, this has a short shelf life as it's naturally brewed and non-pastuerised. Hangover-free. €1 in a shop. 6.2 per cent alcohol. Hangover-free. ★★
Ciechan Porter Drunkenly slurred as 'Cheh-han Porter'	Independently brewed, this small brewery's porter is not so popular in Poland but it is a rare delight for people raised on the black stuff. Much better option than drinking Guinness which is rarely served in its prime state. €0.90 in a shop. 9 per cent alcohol. ★★★★
Ciechan Miodowe Drunkenly slurred as 'Cheh-han Me-o-doh-veh'	A truly delicious beer with real honey in the base of the bottle. Good at any time of the day. Also available as a wheat beer and lager. €1.15 in a shop. 5.4 per cent alcohol. ★★★★★

Beer	Review
Perła Niepasteryowane Drunkenly slurred as 'Per-wah Nee-paster-oh-vah-neh'	A good substitute for Kasztelan. Also from an independent brewery. A little harsher on the tongue but there's no harm in being reminded you're consuming an alcohol not laced with chemicals. €0.80 in a shop. 6 per cent alcohol. ★★★★
Kasztelan Niepasteryowane Drunkenly slurred as 'Cash-teh-lan Nee-paster-oh-vah-neh'	I have a few of these every night as a night cap. Unpasteurised and from an independent brewery. Delicate taste, easy to knock back a dozen before lunch. €0.75 in a shop. 5.7 per cent alcohol. ★★★★
Tyskie Drunkenly slurred as 'Tiss-key-eh'	Widely available on draft, it has your standard beer taste. My favourite of the three big beer names on the Polish market. Easy to slug back but you may have a high piss count with this beer. €0.85 in a shop. 5.7 per cent alcohol ★★★★
Lech Premium Drunkenly slurred as 'Lek'	Popular and cheap beer available in most pubs. SAB Miller were boycotted for a while when they stupidly put up a promotional billboard 'Thirsty for Thrills? Cold Lech' outside Polish president and plane crash victim Lech Kaczynski's final resting place in Wawel Castle, Krakow. €0.85 in a shop. 5.2 per cent alcohol ★★★
Żywiec Porter Drunkenly slurred as 'Jhiv-ee-etz'	If you miss your local pint of Murphys or Guinness, then this is next after Ciechan's porter. Both of these porters are more readily available in stores rather than bars. €1 in a shop. 9.5 per cent alcohol. ★★★★★
Redds Jabłkowy (Apple) Drunkenly slurred as 'Reds Yab-uh-koe-vay'	As close as you'll get to Bulmers, comes in apple and cherry. A little sweet maybe, but if cider is your drink, then this is your saviour. €1 in a shop. 4.5 per cent alcohol. ★★★★

Drinking Tip – Head to your local shop and you'll notice it's also an off-licence. Almost every shop is the same. Buy high grade beer there for next to nothing, tank up in your room, the park (beware of cops) with a few cheap bottles or cans (don't litter the feckin place though) then head to the pub and enjoy the buzz. Alternatively, only sleep two to four hours a night – the drink will catch up with you much quicker. Having said that, I find Poles are big fans of pacing themselves as they like to remember what they did the night before and not wake up tied naked to a lamp-post. Also, they, as should we all, treasure all their organs equally and think we should all love and respect our livers a bit more. If you take extra time off work to celebrate, try not end up like a lad I know, who was fired after his boss saw pictures on Facebook that proved he didn't have an emergency in Warsaw but was, in fact, on a three-day bender.

iii. Survival pub and football Polish

Here are a few Polish signs that will make you scratch your head while certain English words could get you into a lot of trouble if you're not careful.

Here are a few other tips to make sure you don't get off on the wrong foot when speaking to Poles.

• Be careful how you say the word 'Hi' or (say 'H-eye' not 'hoy'), as it's close to the Polish word *chuj* which means dick in English, but it's much stronger in Polish and very offensive.

Arsplay – A well-known children's playground equipment and toy store. Credit: Gabeeg Asiynnek-Dnea

Wankowicz – the name of many streets across Poland as it's the surname of a famous Polish writer. Credit: author

- If you want to ask the questions 'who are you?' or 'how are you?' make sure you stress the 'are' part, otherwise you risk calling a Polish person a 'dickhead'.

- Make sure you pronounce the letter 'r' at the end of 'cheaper' or 'chipper' or 'cheap car', if you pronounce it like 'cheap-ah' or 'chip-ah' it means 'c**t' in Polish.

- If you read the word *cholera*, Poles are not talking about the water-borne disease, rather they are saying 'sh*t' or 'dammit'.

- If you tell a Pole that Irish people or your buddy is a 'lunatic' they'll look at you strangely as it means 'sleep walker' in Polish.

- If a Pole asks you do you have the 'pee-lot', you may think they are asking whether you gotta go to the jacks often. In fact, they are just asking for the remote control.

- You'll notice that the word for wine here is 'wino'. But that means 'dung' in Polish (*łajno*). You shouldn't pronounce it like we'd say 'Your man is a wino'. 'W' in English is pronounced as 'V' in Polish. So you should ask for 'Veen-oh' and then the shop assistant won't piss themselves laughing.

There are some other key things you need to remember in Polish. You may wish to revise them as you take a leak while on the beer, in the back of a taxi to ensure the driver doesn't rip you off, to calm down a heated situation between your friends and any locals, or to impress a local lady or lad.

A pint/half pint of beer please	*Poproszę duże/małe piwo* (Popros-eh do-zhe/mah-weh peevo)
Hello	*Dzień Dobry* (Gin Dough-bray) or Cześć (chaysh-ch)

What's your name?	*Jak masz na imię?* (Yak – mash – na – ee-me-eh)
I'm John	*Jestem Jan* (Yes-tem ____)
Thank you	*Dziękuję* (Jen-koo-yauh)
Sorry/Excuse me	*Przepraszam* (Shay-prash-am)
Where is the jacks?	*Gdzie jest toaleta?* (Ge-jay yest – toe-let-a)
I'm from Ireland	*Jestem z Irlandii* (Yes-tem zeh Ear-land-ee)
I love Poland/Ireland	*Kocham Polskę/Irlandię* (Ko-ham Polsk-auh/Ear-land-e-auh)
Can I have your phone number?	*Dasz mi swój numer telefonu* (Dash-mi ss-foih noo-mer tele-fon-uh)
I'm/You're well-hung	*Jestem/Jesteś dobrze wyposażony* (Yes-tem/Yes-tesh dob-zeh veh-pos-a-zho-nah)
You're a fine bird	*Jesteś piękna* (Yes-tesh pee-en-knah)
The bill please	*Poproszę o rachunek* (Po-prosh-eh oh ra-hoo-nek)
Can I buy you a drink?	*Czy mogę ci postawić piwo?* (Chih moe-gah chee po-sta-veach peevo)
I want to buy	*Chce kupić* – (keh-tseh koo-peach)
Numbers	1 – *yeden* 6 – *shy-shh-ch* 2 – *d-va* 7 – *shedem* 3 – *tre* 8 – *oshe-em* 4 – *shtay-ry* 9 – *jeventch* 5 – *pee-ench* 10 – *jeh-shentch*
No	*Nie*
Yes	*Tak*
Do you speak English? -	*Mówisz po angielsku?* (Moo-veesh po ang-yel-skoo)

Please	*Proszę*
You're welcome	*Proszę* (Prosh-eh)
That's a mistake	*To pomyłka* (Toe Po-may-uh-ka)
I'd like a large/small beer	*Poproszę duże/małe piwo*
Do you have a light?	*Masz fajka?* (Mash fy-kah?)

Useful words

Apteka	Pharmacy
Sklep	Shop
Papierosy	Cigarettes
Bilet	Ticket
Szpital	Hospital
Wezwij karetkę	Call an ambulance
Pociąg	Train
Przystanek	Bus/tram/train stop
Dworzec Głowny	Central Station

Football Polish

When you are watching replays with new Polish friends in the Fan Zones or pub these phrases may come in useful. If you happen to be beside a local football fan during any of the games, he may shout the following:

Football	*Piłka nożna* (puke-ah-noj-nah)
Team	*Drużyna* (droo-zhee-nah)
Goal	*Gol* (gol)
Penalty	*Rzut karny* (jhoot Car-neh)
Foul	*Faul* (foul)

Give the ref a jersey	*Daj sędziemu koszulkę przeciwników* (Die-send-jeh-moo koshulkah preh-chee-nee-kuv)
Offside	*Spalony* (spa-lo-ny)
Corner	*Rzut rożny* (zhoot roo-jny)
Throw in	*Rzucz wolny* (jhooch wolnay)
Free kick	*Rzut wolny* (jhoot wolnay)
Good shot	*Dobry strzał* (do-breh strauh)
Shoot!	*Strzelaj!* (shtrel-ay)
What a miss!	*Jaka strata!* (ya-ka stra-ta)
He's brutal	*On jest okropny* (on yest o-krop-neh)
He's savage	*On jest zajebisty* (on yest zie-eh-beast-eh)
We won	*Wygraliśmy* (vi-gra-lee-shmeh)
It was a draw	*Remis*

iv. Local hangover cures

In fact, it makes sense to start with hangover preventatives. At home we hear tall tales of lining the stomach with a glass of milk. Personally, I always find Choc-Ices and Supersplit icecreams helpful in the summer. During the winter I just buried my head under a pillow after an ice cold shower. Poles have much tested and long-proven methods on how to balance taking a drink and ensuring you don't suffer the consequences. And if you do happen to suffer the consequences, there are a variety of strategies to help revitalise your body.

- *Klin* **(Clean)** – This basically means more alcohol. For us it's the hair of the dog that bit you in the arse. Like the name implies, it means cleaning out the system by numbing it through more intoxication.

In Poland, that commonly means more vodka. Stick with your high quality, more natural beers like Zywe or any non-pasteurised stuff is good.

- *Ogórki* (**Pickles**) – Or marinated cucumbers. You whah?! Well, Poles love 'em. Visit a supermarket and you'll find aisles dedicated to them. Funnily enough, due to their acidic content, they do the job perfectly when you drink large amounts of vodka. If you are a novice to Polish partying, this is a must-eat after each 50 ml shot of vodka has been downed.

- *Kapuśniak* (**Cabbage soup**) – Sour as an arthritis-ridden old woman who sees there is no seat available on the bus. This will do wonders for your ability to speak in a non-slurred manner at 3 a.m. after we hold Spain to a draw or beat the crap out of them.

- *Rosół* – Another miracle hangover cure, in particular chicken broth. You should drink it before a mammoth session to line your stomach. It's a staple part of the traditional Polish diet.

- *Żurek* – A white, sour soup made of rye flour and sour dough, served, believe it or not, with a boiled egg and sausage; tastier than it sounds; it's like Mother Nature personally revamps you with a modern anti-hangover system. This is the soup Irish journalist Tom Galvin was referring to in the title of his book that I mentioned in the intro.

- *Borsch* – Regularly served at 2 a.m. as weddings come to a close, the idea being to sober people up for another onslaught the following day. It's made from beetroot. Stains are a bastard to wash off, so try not get it all over your jersey or you'll look like you were recently knifed.

- *Kefir* – This readily available potion from shops is really just sour milk or, if you want to be semi-scientific, milk with magical bacteria to kill bad stuff going on inside you while you get carried away with our great campaign and over-consume. *Kefir* is often drunk in Central and Eastern Europe the morning after the night before.

7. Dancefloor Tactics and How to Score

Most Poles consume alcohol at each others' homes before going clubbing. They don't have a habit of frequenting pubs for ten hours in advance of chatting up someone and rarely need the courage of intoxication to start dancing. There are loads of great clubs in Poznań and the Tri-City area so you won't have a problem finding entertainment.

Attention Irish men – if you want to win the heart of someone like Polish star Alicja Bachleda-Curuś, then keep the following tips in mind. Credit: David Shankbone, WikiCommons, Creative Commons, Attribution-ShareAlike 3.0 Unported Licence

When a foreigner asks a taxi driver to bring them to a club, it may be interpreted as a strip club or brothel. **Try to know the name and address of where you are going** to avoid getting ripped off or dumped at a 'Hostel' film type party.

If you go to clubs in big groups, with your Irish jerseys reeking of beer and sweat, you may not gain admittance. Many clubs have dress codes and appreciate if people take a bit of time to spruce up. **Casual smart would be your best bet** although most places will probably lighten their rules if you appear sober and loaded.

Of course, **your niche is your Irishness**. It's the same the world over. Have a funny leprechaun hat, jersey or scarf (though it's a bit hot to be wearing at night time). Your pale complexion and sunburnt nose and ears will make you easily identifiable as one of Trap's army. Remember to wear your best Irish fan underpants.

Brush up on your Irish. Many of the girls you'll talk to will have better English than you. So if you introduce yourself by saying *Dia duit, Paddy is ainm dom*, at least you will attract their attention. Then offer to teach them a few phrases – *Is brea liom Poland* (I love Poland) or *Tá grá agam duit/ort* (I love you).

Polish women like their men fairly sober (Polish men like their women sober too. Well, ok, maybe just a little drunk) and don't appreciate drunkards spluttering saliva over them. Grow a pair of balls, believe in yourself and approach a local who has caught your eye when it's early in the night so they can actually hear what you are saying.

Attention Irish women – not all Polish men are built like Mariusz Pudzianówski, who won the world's strongest man competition five times, but they are fairly hulky all the same. Credit: Artur Andrzej, WikiCommons, Creative Commons, Attribution-ShareAlike 3.0 Unported Licence

Remember, if you are from Cork, the North, have a working-class Dublin accent or a bogman's midland accent, fuck all people will understand what you're saying. **Neutralise your accent,** avoid using too much slang, slow down so your audience can understand you. Poles love the Irish accent, but they also want to know what you're skutterin' on about.

Be a listener. Asking lots of questions is a sure bet to get a Pole chatting to you as they can be very reserved at first. **They'll want to practise their English** with you even if they're not at first impressed with your receding hairline.

Make her laugh and praise her to the hilt (Polish women have beautiful eyes, great dress sense and a great sense of humour). Polish guys are built like a five-bedroom dormer.

Talk about Polish people you know in Ireland in a positive light. If you are to have a future together beyond the song 'Stayin Alive', then establishing some early cultural links will be significant. Avoid conversations about road accidents involving Poles in Ireland. Polish people know only too well about tragedies on their own roads.

Remind them that **Ireland is less than a three-hour flight away**, much shorter than the journey from Warsaw to Gdańsk, so if her mum and dad want to visit when you've settled down with five kids, it'll be a cinch.

What the hell is disco polo?

Something a little unique about Polish clubs is **disco polo,** which started in the early 1990s. In the capital Warsaw, it is often looked down on, but it remains very popular among Poles.

It's hard to describe, but it's a bit like Daniel O'Donnell meets DJ Carl Cox and that 1990's German raver Scooter. The ingredients for a disco polo song are not so complex. You need a couple of semi-naked, bad-dancing babes with a chubby 30-something-year-old male, orange in colour from too much time on a sunbed and dressed in a brutal looking Hawaiian cocktail shirt. The lyrics range from a constant repetition of phrases like '*Załóż gumę na instrument*' (Put a condom on the instrument) to 'I've got five 18-year-olds'.

8. Ten Polish Foods Every Fan Should Try

1. *Zapiekanka* **(Toasted baguette)** – The Polish equivalent of Irish deli. rolls. They are everywhere, cheap and will save you from starvation after a marathon three-day session. Toppings are displayed so you don't have to entertain everyone in the queue by pronouncing the menu. Dirt cheap, a godsend when you're suffering from the pangs of hunger.

2. *Pierogi* **(Dumplings)** – The last dumpling to be eaten in Ireland may have been before the famine, but in Poland they are a popular and very tasty dish. Dough stuffed with anything under the sun, they're cheap, filling and can be found everywhere. They have *ruskie* (cottage cheese and potato), *mieso (meat)*, z *kapustą I pieczarkami* (cabbage and mushroom), z *serem* (sweet cheese), z *soczewicą* (lentils), *z szpinakiem i fetą* (with spinach and feta), *z jagodami* (blueberry) and *z truskawkami* (strawberry). In other words, you're spoiled for choice.

3. *Bigos* – Sour cabbage mixed with pieces of pork or sausage, tomato, prunes and, if you're lucky, wine, honey and mushrooms.

4. *Ryby Bałtyckie* **(Baltic fish)** – In Gdańsk, you'll have trawler-full options of deliciously fresh fish like flounder and cod or smoked mackerel. Cheap, healthy and easy to find good quality, it's a great way to reduce your food miles and fill the gap.

5. *Placki ziemniaczane* **(Potato pancakes)** – If you're like me, for the first 21 years of your life you ate roast, mashed, boiled and steamed spuds as well as chips and wedges. These are the Polish version of hash browns, but thinner and tastier. They're either served with sour cream or are sweet.

6. *Flaki* – A morning broth with shredded intestines. Sounds rank but in fact it's nutritious and tasty. Poles drink it during the wake meal after a funeral and they love it. You can get a billion types in shops. This should be left until after any heavy defeats we may endure during the championship.

7. *Schabowy z kapustą i ziemniakami* – Pork chops with cabbage and spuds. One of the most staple and common Polish dishes. Poles love pig meat and are not too keen on beef. This meal will be served everywhere and is as close to our diet as you'll ever get in Poland.

8. *Kabanos* – While Spaniards are munching on the chorizo sausages, we can intimidate them in the stands with a thin, dry but savagely delicious and popular Polish sausage *(kiełbasa)*. They come from hogs (young male pig, fattened with potatoes) in the east of Poland. They last long without getting rank so if you tend to get peckish during sessions have one of these in your bag for good measure. Chewing them in the stadium, we'll get local fans on our side and if the game comes to penalties throwing one on the pitch may put off Xavi enough that he hits the post.

9. *Gofry* – If there is one thing on the Baltic coast that you will see more than men with six-packs and ladies dressed to kill, that is the *gofry*. They are a sweet waffle loaded to the gills with cream, fruit, ice cream. You name it. Anything bound to give you a cardiac arrest within a week, they'll serve it up on an attractive platter.

10. *Poznań pyra* – The symbol of a Poznań local is the *pyra* (spud). They celebrate Pyraland Days in the first half of September but you can eat their traditional food *pyry z gzikiem* (potatoes with cottage cheese) and *plyndze* (hash browns) at any time.

(For foods that help with alcohol consumption refer to the **'Hangover Cures'** section in Chapter 6.)

9. Getting Value for Money

In spring/summer 2012 €1 is good value at 4.25 złoty (zwauh-teh). Remember that 100 groszy (grosh-eh) = 1 zł and 1 zł = around €0.25.

Coins are in 1, 2, 5, 10, 20, 50 groszy and 1, 2, 5 zł. Notes are in 10, 20, 50, 100, 200 denominations. Always have small changes and notes with you as most shops just won't serve you if you try to buy a packet of chewing gum for 100 zł.

Money exchange offices are called *kantors*. You'll get a worse deal in banks at home, in *kantors* at the airport or tourist hotspots. A few good ones can be found here in Poznań (ul. 27 Grudnia 9, ul. Polwiejska 42, Plac Wolnosci 14, ul. Glogowska 18, or the Railway Station Main Hall, Dworcowa 1) and in Gdańsk (Al. Grunwaldzka 141, Gdańsk (Galeria Bałtycka) and the city centre has some good rates, but you can also easily check banks like Pekao SA and Millennium).

Cost of living in Poland

Some of these may help you budget and give you an idea whether you are being ripped off. Others are for general interest so you can compare them with how things are at home. When it comes to property, the law of supply and demand means prices are inflated by up to 30 per cent of what they should be.

Cheap meal in a milk (*mleczny*) bar	€3
Three-course meal for two (mid-range)	€20
Fast food meal	€3.50
Beer in a shop	€0.75–1.00
Beer in a pub	€2–€3
Tea	€1.30
Cappuccino	€2
White Bread (500g)	€0.75
Eggs (10)	€2
Fresh cheese (1kg)	€5.50
Water (1.5l)	€0.50
Three-month public transport ticket	€45
Petrol per litre	€1.20
Diesel per litre	€1
Monthly electricity, gas, water, rubbish	€67
Internet (6 mbps, flat rate, cable/ADSL)	€13
Monthly fitness club fee	€30
Cinema ticket	€5
Pair of Levi 501s	€60
Summer dress from Zara	€30
Nike runners	€60
Men's leather shoes	€65
1–3 bedroom apartment, monthly rent in city centre	€350–600
1–3 bedroom apartment, monthly rent outside centre	€250–450

Apartment prices	per square metre in city centre	€1,840
	per square metre outside centre	€1,265
Average net monthly salary		€620
Red wine (750ml)		€5
Smirnoff vodka (700ml)		€7
Cigarettes		€2-3
Newspaper		€0.50
Durex condoms (12)		€7
Energizer batteries AA (4)		€2
Nurofen Ultra, 10 pills		€2.90
Colgate toothpaste (75ml)		€2.25
Potatoes (1kg)		€0.95
Bananas (1kg)		€1.30
Apples (1kg)		€0.90
Oranges (1kg)		€1.20
Orange/Cola (2 litre)		€1.20
Juice (1l)		€0.80
Milk (1l)		€0.65
Fresh chicken breast (1kg)		€4.65

Sources: Personal shopping habits & numbeo.com

10. Fan Embassies and Consulates

You have arrived in Poznań or Gdańsk, or maybe you're taking a break from the football to sightsee Warsaw or Krakow. You've always been known as one for getting lost, needing help to find your bearings, even when you are pulling out of your own driveway. Where's the stadium? The toilet? Your hotel room key? Your underpants?

Don't sweat, fan embassies and consulates are here to help. They are run by fans and for fans. They'll give you more ideas about what to do and see in the city, help you look for accommodation, put you in touch with local fans, help you if you've lost anything of value or your passport. There'll be stationary and mobile stands for Irish fans in Poznań and Gdańsk and wherever else we end up playing.

They probably won't find you a wife, husband, drugs or free tickets, but for general football and tourist-related matters they'll be a lifeline.

A series of workshops have already been held with representatives from the qualifying teams' supporters' clubs. Darek Łapiński of PL.2012 is one of the co-ordinators. During one of these workshops Robert

Pękała of the Poznań City Hall Crisis Management and Security Department was quoted as saying, 'the police will be tolerant of the conduct typical of great football events. People acting noisily due to joy or emotions are not a threat as a rule. Drunken behaviour does not necessarily cause danger, but if it results in a breach of peace, the police will react.'

All those representing the fan embassis will have IDs and recognisable t-shirts. Ambassadors are all volunteers, are over 18 years old, speak at least one foreign language and will be at train stations, airports and tourist information points to give you directions, help with accommodation problems and attend to medical care, while also being engaged in behind-the-scenes work with media support for the city councils.

11. Euro 2012 Team Base Camps

Sopot's Sheraton Hotel will play host to the Irish squad for the duration of the championship. Credit: www.sheraton.pl

Maybe you'd like to see the boys in green putting their final touches together or see how Trap struts his stuff on the pitch. Well, the FAI supposedly visited fifteen options in Poland and the Ukraine before deciding on the Sheraton Sopot Hotel.

It's 16 km from the city centre of Gdańsk along Al. Grunwaldzka (Grunwald Avenue). It's a gorgeous area and a real point scored to have it for our team's preparations. It can also be easily reached by SKM trains that depart from Sopot just 7 km away. Hopefully our lads won't get lured off into the bushes and over-worked by some of the tanned beach blondes or twist an ankle playing beach soccer.

Ireland's training ground is at the new Municipal Stadium in Gdynia (Stadion GOSiR). Try to make it there and offer them support if you can. Credit: Marcin Nasieniewski, WikiCommons, Creative Commons, Attribution-ShareAlike 3.0 Unported, 2.5 Generic, 2.0 Generic and 1.0 Generic Licence

Directions to the stadium (see Map 8): Head north on Al. Niepodległości toward Jakuba Goyki 2.4 kms and then another 3.6kms on Al. Zwycięstwa. Turn left onto Stryjska street and at Węzeł Macieja Brzeskiego, take the 2nd exit onto Małokacka before turning right onto Olimpijska. The stadium is on your right.

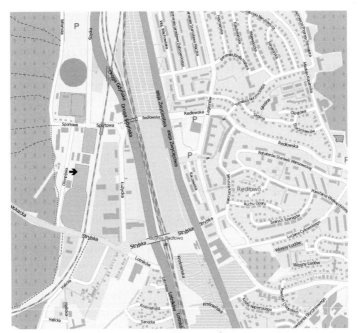

Map 8: Map of the area where you can find the Municipal Stadium in Gdynia. Credit: © www.OpenStreetMap.org contributors, CC BY-SA 3.0. © www.ump.waw.pl contributors, CC BY-SA 3.0

The capacity of the stadium is 15,000. It has top class gym facilities and is sure to get our lads primed for their big battles in Group C. There should be no bother getting access to parts of the training so keep abreast through the ybig.ie Facebook page or their forums and someone is bound to give updated info. on what times they are training.

If you fancy checking out Spain, Germany or Denmark, they are also based in the Tri-City area, whereas Portugal will be staying and prepping in Poznań. Croatia have decided to base themselves in Warsaw while Italy are further south in Group A's host city, Wroclaw. A trip to the beautiful city of Krakow will allow you see Italy, England and the Netherlands strut their stuff. Here's a full list of the teams' hotels and training grounds.

Team	Hotel	Training base (nearest host city)
Croatia	Hotel Sielanka, Warka	Training Ground Sielanka, Warka (Warsaw)
Czech Republic	Hotel Monopol, Wroclaw	Municipal Stadium Oporowska Wroclaw (Wroclaw)
Denmark	Hotel Marine, Kolobrzeg	Municipal Stadium Kolobrzeg, Kolobrzeg (Gdansk)
England	Stary Hotel, Krakow	Hutnik Stadium, Krakow (Wroclaw)
Spain	Hotel Mistral Sport, Groewino	Municipal Stadium Gniewino, Gniewino (Gdansk)
France	Kirsha Training Facility, Donetsk	Kirsha Training Facility (Donetsk)
Germany	Hotel Dwor Oliwski, Gdansk	Municipal Sport Centre Gdansk (Gdansk)
Greece	Hotel Warszawianka Wellness & Spa, Serock	Municipal Stadium Legionowo, Legionowo (Warsaw)
Republic of Ireland	Sheraton Sopot Hotel, Sopot	Municipal Stadium Gdynia, Gdynia (Gdansk)

(Continued)

11. Euro 2012 Team Base Camps

(Continued)

Team	Hotel	Training base (nearest host city)
Italy	Turowka Hotel & Spa. Wieliczka	Municipal Stadium Cracovia, Krakow (Wroclaw)
Netherlands	Sheraton Krakow Hotel, Krakow	Municipal Stadium Wisla Krakow (Wroclaw)
Poland	Hyatt Regency Warsaw, Warsaw	Municipal Stadium Polonia Warszawa (Warsaw)
Portugal	Hotel Remes Sport & Spa, Opalenica	Municipal Stadium Opalenica, Opalenica (Poznań)
Russia	Hotel Meridian Bristol, Warsaw	Municipal Stadium Sulejowek, Sulejowek (Warsaw)
Sweden	Platium Hotel, Kozyn	Koncha Zaspa Training Centre (Kyiv)
Ukraine	Dynamo Kyiv Training Center, Kyiv	Dynamo Kyiv Training Centre (Kyiv)

Source: www.uefa.com

12. Fan Zones

The first official Fan Zone during UEFA champion-ships took place in Portugal in 2004, following on from the massive numbers of people who turned out on the streets of Seoul to watch the World Cup in 2002. During the 2006 World Cup in Germany the Fan Zones were visited by more than 14 million people.

Maybe you'll be too cash-trapped to splash out for a Category A €120 + admin. fee of €10 + resale charge of 10 per cent = €142, all just for a 90-minute game of 22 rich men kicking around a ball. After all, that's almost the weekly wage of people on the dole in Ireland and the monthly sum a Polish person receives if they are out of work.

Maybe you'd rather just soak up the atmosphere, the sunrays and try your hand at scoring or having the craic with a Polish fan. Without a doubt, Fan Zones are the second best place after the stadium to experi-ence the championship. There'll be all the other games, highlights and all sorts of other entertainment, so make sure you get there.

In Poznań you'll find it at Plac Wolności (Freedom Square) (see Map 9), while in Gdańsk it's at Plac Zebrań

Ludowych (People's Gathering Square). If you are in Poland early enough, then it's there that you wanna be watchin' Poland's opening game against Greece on 8 June and catching up with what's hot and what's not for Euro 2012. If you intend on letting your hair down to your ankles while here, then make sure you are semi and merrily tanked up before you hit the Zone and bring a catheter bag or plastic bottle to pee in, as no alcohol is allowed inside the Zone and portaloos are bound to be busy and stinkin' due to the heat and high water consumption.

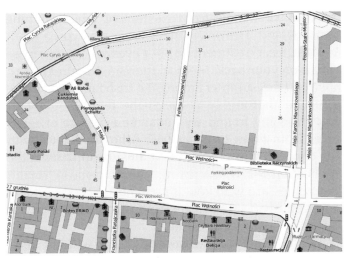

Map 9: Poznań's Fan Zone will be located at Plac Wolności (Freedom Place) just west of the Old Town market square. Credit: www.poznan.pl

Entry is free and there'll be thousands of fans present watching the games live on the big screen and partying to the extra entertainment – mostly Polish acts but we've been promised a few surprises too – maybe Richie Kavanagh will hit the stage with a bit of *aon focail eile*, so have a few eggs handy. You're going to hear lots of good Polish music, and also lots of junk, but who cares when you're half-cut, half-naked and soaking up the sunshine and enjoying the party vibe.

Free medical care will be available, which might come in handy if you ran into a few walls on the way home the night before. Fan Zone maps will spell out where everything is. Ambulances will also be at hand to cart you to the hospital in case you faint from the heat, or maybe from excitement when Ukraine beat England. However, they won't give you a tooth implant, laser treatment on your eyes or wax that mass of hair on your back. Medical tourism is bound to be a hot trend this summer among the Irish fans – just make sure you thoroughly research the dentist or doctor you are going to and try get some evidence of references from Poles or other Irish who have been with any clinics you are considering. Ensure you fill out the application for/renew/bring your European Health Insurance Card with you. It's a handy process and will save you financial hardship upon return home if you face an accident while abroad.

Alcohol and mind-blowing drugs will be dealt with in a **zero-tolerance** fashion, i.e. cops will rob and make good use of them. Be warned – you'll only get into these Zones after you and your bags have been frisked. If the frisker is good-looking you may want to act very suspiciously so they give you a good rub down. In case you happen to have a crate of Poland's version of Dutch Gold on your shoulder when you want to enter the Zone, remember that the free deposit areas available are not designed for such big loads.

There will be **four outdoor screens** in the Poznań Fan Zone, the main one being 100 m². As planned, the stage will host concerts, animations for youngsters and other attractions. The outdoor screen, outside match transmission times, will become a summer cinema. The other screens will be along Marcinkowski Avenue.

1,000 seats in two stands will be located next to the stage so if you plan on being there for a long time grab a seat. The Fan Zone will have a capacity of up to 30,000 in total though they'll probably curb this to 20–25,000 for safety reasons. When matches are on in Poznań, opening times are from 12 (noon) to 2 a.m., and from three hours before kick off until midnight on days Poznań is not hosting games. The Fan Zone project has planned 160 portaloos so taking a leak shouldn't be a problem. There'll be lots of **catering stands** with grub and drink, entertainment stands, an official sponsor shop, security services and press centre – and for the snobs a paid VIP zone.

The stadium in Poznań is 7 km and the main railway station 2 km from the Fan Zone while the Old Market is just 0.5 km away. Bring a backpack with you with 2 litres of water, sun lotion, a good hat, shades, rehydration salts, headache tablets, a handkerchief, a few sambos or dry foods or fruit to avoid extortionate prices likely to cream you in and around the Zone. Be super careful in the Zones as regards your wallet, phone and passport. Carry everything to your front and not in your arse pocket. Reserve that space for this guide. Pickpockets amongst 30,000 fans are a dead cert., so don't give them any reason to swarm towards your group. Bumbags are a good way to secure your valuables, while not wearing any deodorant will create such a natural rank odour it's bound to prove a lethal deterrent.

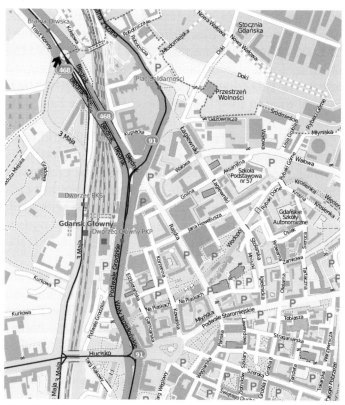

Map 10: Gdańsk Fan Zone. Credit: © www.OpenStreetMap.org contributors, CC BY-SA 3.0. © www.ump.waw.pl contributors, CC BY-SA 3.0

The Fan Zone in Gdańsk (see Map 10) in Plac Zebrań Ludowych (People's Gathering Square) is located on 44,000 square metres so chances you'll lose your mates are quite high unless you've got Polish SIM cards to keep in touch or a handy rendezvous point. The central train and bus stations are 0.5 km away, the SKM train (Rapid Urban Railway Line), which services the Tri-City area, is next to it, the city centre about 1.5 km and the airport over 12 km away. All the games will be screened live while music with Polish and foreign stars will be aplenty. Aleja Zwycięstwa is located next to the square so buses, trams and car transport can easily access the Zone. It's 40 minutes from the stadium.

Medical foot patrols in red uniforms will be at hand if you need any treatment and ambulances will be on standby. Bags and clothes will be checked on the way in so make sure you've got no drugs, alcohol, semi-automatic weapons, endangered species or smelly armpits. Make sure you get a receipt for whatever items you deposit.

13. Placing Bets in Poland

The Polish football association (PZPN – Polski Związek Piłki Nożnej) and Polish politicians declared war on internet gambling a couple of years ago out of concerns about gambling addiction and other social problems. Slot machines were restricted to officially-registered casinos.

The three biggest bookmakers are Totolek, STS and Professional. They have 1,000+ bookmaker shops all over the country. There's a 10 per cent tax levied on your winnings but despite this and online gambling being illegal, the industry is thriving. There are no internet restrictions to block web users from entering foreign betting websites so you'll have no problem in that regard. See Euro 2012 Groups in the colour photo section for Boyle Sports odds on outright winner betting.

In Poznań the best spot to put on a bet is Millennium bookmakers (*zakłady bukmacherskie*) on ul. Kraszewsk-iego or MAX S.A., which you will find around the city. They'll be able to speak enough English to help you fill out the form.

In Gdańsk, the major bookmakers have outlets so check them out, set yourself a limit and test your predictive skills.

Most of the main Irish bookmakers are also likely to have a presence around our games so keep an eye on their website for special mobile phone betting deals for Irish fans. Of course, if you're going to be betting via your mobile phone while in Poland, you'll save yourself a packet on roaming charges if you pick up a local SIM card starter pack. See Final Top Ten Tips at the end of the book for more details.

14. Poland in Brief

Poland is about four and a half times the size of Ireland and has a population that dwarfs ours – 39 million. But for World War II, the population would stand at possibly twice that today. One-third of Poland's population were killed between 1939 and 1945 as a result of the conflict and systematic genocide.

But let's wind back the clock. Every year on Easter Monday Poles have a funny tradition of drenching each other with water to celebrate Śmyngus Dyngus, recalling how the Polish nation accepted Christianity in the year 966. Their acceptance of Christianity has played a massive role in the country's history ever since.

In the 14th century the country entered a union with Lithuania, which lasted until the very end of the 18th century. The union made Poland one of the strongest states in Europe, until the ruling Jagiellon dynasty began losing control over the increasingly determined nobility. The Polish Parliament, the Sejm, became the main legislative power in the middle of the 16th century. After the death of the last Jagiellon king in 1569, Poland became an elective monarchy, a

With loyal fans like these, how could you go far wrong? Skopje, Macedonia, 4 June 2011.
Credit: John Barrington/nineteen21

Euro 2012 Groups: Kits, Coaches and Boyle Sports Odds

Group A (Warsaw/Wroclaw)

	Poland	Greece	Russia	Czech Rep.
Kit (Home/Away)				
Captain/Coach	Jakub Błaszczykowski/ Franciszek Smuda	Giorgos Karagounis/ Fernando Santos	Andrei Arshavin/ Dick Advocaat	Tomáš Rosický/ Michal Bílek
Boyle Sports Odds	50/1	66/1	20/1	50/1

Group B (Kharkiv/Lviv)

	Germany	Netherlands	Portugal	Denmark
Kit (Home/Away)				
Captain/ Coach	Philipp Lahm/ Joachim Löw	Mark van Bommel/ Bert van Marwijk	Cristiano Ronaldo/ Paulo Bento	Daniel Agger/ Morten Olsen
Boyle Sports Odds	10/3	18/1	18/1	80/1

Group C (Gdańsk/Poznan)

	Spain	Italy	Rep. of Ireland	Croatia
Kit (Home/Away)				
Captain/Coach	Iker Casillas/ Vincente del Bosque	Cesare Prandelli/ Gianluigi Buffon	Robbie Keane/ Giovanni Trapattoni	Dario Srna/ Slavek Bilic
Boyle Sports Odds	5/2	14/1	80/1	40/1

Group D (Kiev/Donetsk)

	England	France	Sweden	Ukraine
Kit (Home/Away)				
Captain/Coach	Stuart Pearce/ Scott Parker	Hugo Lloris/ Laurent Blanc	Zlatan Ibrahimović/ Erik Hamrén	Andriy Shevchenko/ Oleh Blokhin
Boyle Sports Odds	9/1	14/1	80/1	40/1

Republic of Ireland team, Aviva Stadium, 29 February 2012.

Back row (L to R): Sean St Ledger, Darren O'Dea, Stephen Ward, Glenn Whelan, Keith Andrews, John O'Shea.

Front row (L to R): Aiden McGeady, Shay Given, Robbie Keane (c), Damien Duff, Shane Long.

Croatia team v Sweden, Zagreb, 29 February 2012.
Back Row (L to R): Josip Simunic, Vedran Corluka, Gordon Schildenfeld, Mario Mandzukic, Tomislav Dujmovic, Stipe Pletikosa. Front Row (L to R): Darijo Srna, Domagoj Vida, Luka Modric, Ivan Rakitic, Ivica Olic.

Credit: Getty Images

Spain team v Venezuela, Málaga, 29 February 2012.

Back row (L to R): Iker Casillas, Sergio Ramos, Xabi Alonso, Sergio Busquets, Gerard Pique, Fernando Llorente.

Front row (L to R): Cesc Fabregas, David Silva, Álvaro Arbeloa, Andrés Iniesta, Jordi Alba.

Credit: Getty Images

Italy team v USA, Genoa, 29 February 2012.
Back row (L to R): Andrea Barzagli, Angelo Ogbonna, Christian Maggio, Thiago Motta, Allesandro Matri, Gianluigi Buffon (c).
Front row (L to R): Antonio Nocerino, Claudio Marchisio, Domenico Criscito, Andrea Pirlo, Sebastian Giovinco.
Credit: Getty Images

Keano celebrates his fifty-first international goal and Ireland's 0–2 victory in Macedonia.
Credit: John Barrington/nineteen21

Macedonia 0–2 Republic of Ireland, Skopje, 4 June 2011. It was a night to treasure in more ways than one for our legendary captain Robbie Keane (pictured). After eight minutes he bagged the opener and his second a half hour later wrote him into the history books. Keano had become the first Irish international to score over 50 goals for his country.

Credit: John Barrington/nineteen21

Irish boss Giovanni Trapattoni shows off his skills at the Republic of Ireland v Poland game, November 2008.
Credit: John Barrington/nineteen21

Jon Walters celebrates after scoring his first international goal, in our away qualifying match against Estonia, while our opening goal scorer Keith Andrews gets ready to chase after him.

Credit: John Barrington/nineteen21

The mighty Shay Given plucks another one from the sky to deny the Estonians a consolation prize.
Credit: John Barrington/nineteen21

FAI Senior Player of the Year Richard Dunne.
Credit: John Barrington/nineteen21

Giovanni Trapattoni celebrated his 70th birthday on St Patrick's Day 2009. Here he is enjoying his Irish birthday party with a young fan.
Credit: John Barrington/nineteen21

Republic of Ireland management team – Liam Brady, Giovanni
Trapattoni and Marco Tardelli.
Credit: John Barrington/nineteen21

Members of the Irish supporter's club (You Boys in Green) made a
recent trip to Poland where they received a great reception, meeting
the mayors of Gdańsk and Poznań, staying at The Sheraton which will
serve as the Irish team's hotel, getting tours of the various stadia and
generally experiencing typical Polish hospitality. Such pre-game trips lay
the foundations for positive relations when Irish fans travel abroad.
Credit: John Barrington/nineteen21

Irish Fans go mental in Tallinn, Estonia. Deservedly so as we were victorious 0–4, paving the way to Euro 2012.
Credit: John Barrington/nineteen21.

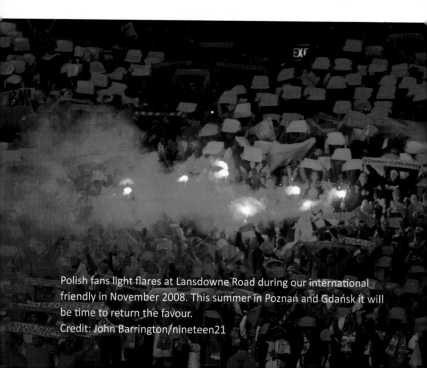

Polish fans light flares at Lansdowne Road during our international friendly in November 2008. This summer in Poznań and Gdańsk it will be time to return the favour.
Credit: John Barrington/nineteen21

quasi-democratic state in an era of absolute monarchies all around Europe. The 1683 Battle of Vienna won by Jan Sobieski III is credited as having saved Christianity in Europe from the spread of Islam.

The once powerful state gradually fell to stronger neighbours in the 17th and 18th century, and was partitioned by the Austrian Hapsburg Empire in the south, the Prussians in the west and the Russians in the east. Poles are credited with having introduced the first constitution in Europe and, as regards tolerance and intercultural living, are regarded as being miles ahead of the rest of Europe. The idea of Polish independence was kept alive through the 19th century, by writers such as Adam Mickiewicz, Henryk Sienkiewicz and others.

Poland regained its independence after World War I for two decades, but was tragically sandwiched and partitioned between Hitler's Nazi Germany and Stalin's Soviet Russia in September 1939. Many thousands of Poles served in the armies of the Allied forces and, of all the warring countries, it was Poland that lost the highest ratio of its citizens. During the war, 6 million Polish citizens were killed by Germans and 2.5 million transported to labour or extermination camps. In all, one-fifth of the population perished (half of them Jewish) and Poland lost 20 per cent of its former land after the war ended.

After World War II, Poland became a satellite state of the Soviet Union. Uprisings in Poznań in 1956 and anti-censorship/regime marches in 1968 were brutally suppressed. In 1978, Karol Wojtyła became Pope John Paul II. In 1989, led by a reformist trade union movement called Solidarity, and eight years after martial law was first introduced, Poland became the first eastern European state to break free of Communism.

The economy of Poland developed into one of the most robust in Eastern Europe, being the only EU country not to experience negative growth in recent years. Poland joined NATO on 27 May 1999 and the European Union on 1 May 2004; it joined Schengen in 2007.

It held the presidency of the EU in the second half of 2011 and Euro 2012 is the first time a major football championship has been held in the country. Among the famous Polish names you may recognise are composer Frederyk Chopin, film director Roman Polanski, boxer Andrzej Gołota, ski-jumper Adam Małysz, cross-country skiing champion Justyna Kowalczyk, Formula One driver Robert Kubica and *Goldeneye* Bond girl Izabella Scorupco.

15. Polish Football History

Gregorz Lato (right), seen pictured with UEFA President Michel Patini, scored Poland's winning goal against Brazil in their '74 World Cup encounter. He is currently head of the Polish FA.
Credit: Klearchos Kapoutsis, WikiCommons, Creative Commons, Attribution-ShareAlike 2.0 Generic Licence

The Polish Football Association was set up in 1919, a year after Poland gained its independence. Poland's footballing heydays were in the 1970s and 80s, winning gold at the 1972 Olympics, silver in 1976 and 1992. They finished third in both the 1974 and 1982 World Cups.

They have qualified for the World Cup seven times, but the first time they took part in the European Championships was in 2008. The premier league in Poland is called T-Mobile Ekstraklasa and was started in 1927.

Since the end of Communism in 1989, the dominating clubs have been Legia Warszawa (won the premier title nine times but were stripped of one title due to corruption) and Wisła Krakow (fourteen titles). Gornik Zabrze have also won fourteen titles and they lost 2–1 to Manchester City in the UEFA Cup Winners cup final in 1970. Legia Warsaw were in the semi-final. Ruch Chorzow have won thirteen times. Lech Poznań, in whose home stadium we're going to annihilate the Croatians and Italians, have won the Polish league six times, lastly in 2010.

In recent seasons, several Polish clubs have been found guilty of corruption and fined, deducted points or even relegated as a result. Over 200 referees, coaches and players have been arrested in recent years as well as officials from the Polish Football Association (PZPN).

The current head of the PZPN is Gregorz Lato, Poland's record goalscorer and a key player in their 1970s success. He won the Golden Boot with his seven goals in the 1974 World Cup, scoring their winning goal against Brazil to earn his side third place. Poland are currently ranked 75 by FIFA.

One of their greatest players over the past two decades has undoubtedly been long-time Celtic keeper, Artur Boruc. But we have to dip further into

Poland's past to find their greatest ever player – Kazimierz Deyna. Nicknamed *Rogal* (croissant), his shots swerved like a rally driver. He played with Manchester City at the end of the 1980s. If you're a film buff, you might remember him from the 1981 film *Escape to Victory* where he played Paul Wolcheck. He died in a car accident in 1989 at the age of just 41. Sadly, Polish football recently lost another of its legends, Włodzimierz Smolarek, at just 54. A former Polish international footballer, he was capped 60 times for the Polish national team and was a member of the 1982 FIFA World Cup squad that came in third place.

Unfortunately for Poland's current side, both Łukasz Podolski and Mirosłav Klose (2006 World Cup Golden Boot winner and joint second with Gerd Müller on the list of FIFA's World Cup goalscorers, having scored fourteen goals) were born in Poland but chose to play for Germany.

16. Ukraine in Brief

Ukraine has endured spells under both Russian and Lithuanian rule. It is the second biggest country in Europe and is seven and a half times bigger than Ireland. It has a population of 46 million, so about ten times bigger than the Republic. They converted to Christianity in 988, just 22 years after the Poles. They were annexed by Poland and Lithuania in the 14th century and partitioned between Poland and Russia in 1667.

The Ukrainian language was banned under the Russian empire from 1793. A short period of independence (1917–1922) was followed again by Russian (east) and Polish (west) dominance. Poet and artist Taras Shevchenko (1814–1861) is a national hero and, as you well know, he has an easy surname to remember. Stalinist Russia imposed a system of collective farms that lead to famine in 1932–1933, which killed 3–7 million Ukrainians. They regained independence in 1991, having been controlled by Soviet Russia since the end of World War II. The Chernobyl nuclear disaster in 1986 helped expose the failures of Soviet Russian rule.

In 2004 the Ukraine saw a massive and mainly peaceful political upheaval during the 'Orange Revolution'. It occurred after the main opposition called into question the legitimacy of general election results that had seen a pro-Kremlin candidate, Vikthor Janukovich, returned to power despite growing popular sentiment for the more pro-western leadership under Viktor Yushchenko (since then half-clobbered by an alleged poison attack) and Julia Tymoshenko (now in prison).

Following the Orange Revolution, on 26 December 2004, after two rounds of falsified elections, Yushchenko beat the Kremlin-backed candidate in the third round of voting. Under Yushchenko, pro-westerners rejoiced saying that the Ukraine had finally become free from Moscow's 300-year domination. Their honeymoon was short-lived though, as the reins of power went back to the other side within two years. Since then, all three have been playing political tennis while the public have by and large stepped back to cope with the harsh realities of relatively poor public sector wages and a generally unstable economic climate. It might be hard for you to believe, but the average Ukrainian earns just €237 per month, or in Euro 2012 terms the equivalent of category one and category two tickets to their own qualifying games in Group D.

We Irish have something very dark in common with the Ukraine and it's not the colour of our favourite drink. In November 2008, the IMF approved a €12 billion bailout package to stabilise their banking system and offset the dire consequences of a massive collapse in the price of steel, one of its main exports.

Sounds familiar, doesn't it? In fact, we got €10 billion more from the IMF in our 2010 bailout, which was a quarter of our total €85 billion package. I better stop there as I'm already beginning to grind my teeth.

The Ukraine usually only makes international news nowadays when the extraordinarily attractive feminist group Femem bare almost all in stunts designed to draw attention to the treatment of Ukrainian women for the purposes of prostitution and human trafficking. Euro 2012 has been the subject of their wrath recently for this very same reason. Ukrainian authorities themselves came under scathing criticism recently from animal rights activists, football fans, UEFA and even a number of international German football players. According to animal rights activists from PETA Germany, up to 20,000 stray dogs may have been put down to clear up the paths and roads for Euro 2012 visitors.

17. Ukrainian Football History

Gaining independence in 1991, Ukraine played their first match, against Hungary, in 1992. Prior to this their players made up a large part of the USSR team. They didn't qualify for any major tournament before 2005, Croatia denying them a place in the 1998 FIFA World Cup and Slovenia from going to Euro 2000. Germany ruined their quest for the 2002 FIFA World Cup.

Under the stewardship of Ukrainian Oleg Blokhin they reached their first-ever FIFA World Cup in 2006 but were annihilated by Spain 4–0, though they beat Tunisia and Saudi Arabia in their other games. Defeating Switzerland on penalties they reached the quarter-finals before losing 3–0 to Italy, who went on to the win the championship.

Former Chelsea and AC Milan star Shevchenko now plays for Dynamo Kyiv and his national side as a striker. He is the third-highest scorer in the history of European club competition with 67 goals. Scoring 175 goals scored with AC Milan, he became the second highest goalscorer in the history of the Italian club. He has netted 46 goals in 108 caps for the Ukraine's national football team.

In 2003 the Ukrainian captain won the UEFA Champions League with AC Milan. Only three Ukrainians (Shevchenko, current Ukranian coach Oleg Blokhin and Igor Belanov) have won the Ballon d'Or football award; Shevchenko captured the accolade in 2004. And he has also won various league and cup titles in Ukraine, Italy, and England.

He played an inspiring captain's role in leading the Ukraine six years ago to the quarter-finals in their first-ever FIFA World Cup. This is very likely to be his last major competition and I, for one, am looking forward to him scoring five goals against England and handling the ball into the French net.

18. Safety and Security

i. Hooliganism

You can be fairly rest-assured that you will not witness any hooliganism during the championships due to the security precautions being put in place. Having said that, we all remember that it's just three years ago since Polish hooligans clashed on the streets of Belfast before a friendly with Northern Ireland that ended in a 3–2 victory for the home side. Six years ago, before the Germany World Cup, every one thought Polish, English and German hooligans would run riot. In fact, little happened apart from 300 arrests made in Dortmund after drunken Polish and German fans clashed.

The history of Polish hooliganism is much darker, organised and fatal than ever existed in England. Dozens of deaths have resulted from mindless violence between competing 'firms'. Hooligans are a bizarre bunch – often anti-semitic, xenophobic yet with strict codes depending on what clubs they belong to.

And sometimes their members go mainstream and become professional boxers, like rising heavyweight star and former hooligan jailbird, Artur Szpilka. But all in all, hooligans are a tiny minority, and it's important to remember that some Polish and other team sports even have their own pilgrimages to holy sites in Poland.

Krakow's hooligan scene is the most notorious and violent, whereas Warsaw's clubs pre-arrange their fights out of public view, have a more disciplined no weapons pact and battle it out together in forests. It has also been linked with the control of territories in the city for drug distribution.

For Euro 2012 on-the-spot trials and penalties for those involved in fighting will be done via video-conference in stadiums. Holding cells have been constructed in the stadia to keep them under wraps. So how to avoid trouble – well, keep your head up, your eyes and ears open, your mouth shut and run like hell if a fights break out. This is a highly unlikely scenario in the Poznań and Gdańsk stadium, but be vigilant around Fan Zones and in the city centre for drunken louts or at other teams' games.

ii. Tickets, touts and tossers

You and I, we may already have something quite important in common. Have you spent hours on end refreshing the game page of the most annoying website ever created by humankind? Yup, that's right, your addiction to UEFA's ticket portal has killed more of your brain cells in the past couple of months than a lifetime of porter could ever do.

At the time of writing I've scored four Category A tickets for both Spain and Croatia. I eventually grabbed three Italy tickets after two and half months of computer gazing and, immediately after that, I declared my retirement from sitting in front of the UEFA portal all day. UEFA-portal-coholism has become a grave addiction for Irish fans and is said to be the main catalyst in young Irish men and women losing their hair, growing a belly, rowing with their spouse and forgetting they have children!

Euro 2012 – over 1.4 million tickets, 31 matches and half a million fans. But even as Michel Platini was launching ticket sales in Warsaw, tout websites were already selling for the games. John Delaney was quoted as saying in the *Irish Examiner* at the beginning of the year that 25–30,000 Irish fans would travel to Poland. But we were only designated 6,000 tickets and even those dedicated fans who travelled all over the gaffe to see the boys play abroad in the qualifiers have to wait and hope. Meanwhile, touts are buying up tickets and selling them on at a hefty profit. Wheeling and dealing online and on the ground once ya get here is a key component of the filthy rotten ticketing system we are forced to endure.

Within days of resales on UEFA's website, websites were charging as much as five times the actual price. If you haven't got a ticket for the game, rather than feeding touts heaps of money and risking getting scammed outside stadiums, just head to the Fan Zones. They're definitely going to be great craic too, you'll probably see more action, will save a lot of dosh and have a better chance of chatting up a local.

If you buy online outside of the official UEFA channel, check whether the supplier has an address, phone and company registration number, or a history of operating online (google their website name). If the prices are too good to be true, they are probably duds. Do they have a real looking ticket number? Don't be taken in by an over-friendly voice and prompt email responses that are selling tickets at or below face value. Forged tickets outside the stadium are a certainty. In the past, during major championships, tickets have sold for up to 30 times their original cost. So if you're going to buy in desperation, first know exactly how a real ticket feels and looks like.

Over the past few days, I've had some email correspondence with touts to see what the hell they were up to and how much they were charging. There was a thread on polishforums.com where lots of these scumbags came out of the woodwork and tried to pawn their paper gold. My fake email name was John and I had the following correspondence with the first tout:

Me: What category is the Ireland–Croatia game? How much will you sell them for? How can I use them if they are not in my name? I heard that in March the person who buys needs to write the names of the people who are going to use the tickets. So If I buy them from you, will you take a screenshot of the application where you have entered my name? How am I going to get the tickets from you?

Tout 1 (Martin): Hi John, I personally never heard of this name changing thing. I have been to the World Cup in Germany in 2006 and Euro 2008 and they *never* checked the tickets for names. I doubt they will do it in Poland. Tickets are CAT 1 – I'm based in London for cash exchange – alternatively can meet in Poland – will be in Warsaw from the 7th June. 2 tickets for Ireland will be £500.

Martin

Me: Jaysus man, that's steep, I thought you just wanted them off your hands. Fair enough, face value's out the window, but Christ, any scope for a bit of perspective here. I'm a big Irish fan. Can't be spending all day on the portal coz I've got kids and demanding but shite paying work. You willing to come down from double the price?

Cheers, J.

Tout 1: Hi John, Sorry but that's my price. I'm trying to get my hands on the opening game (2 tickets) Poland v Greece but tickets are being sold for over £500 per ticket!!!! Unfortunately, it's a lethal chain! I will definitely get ripped off myself further down the line. These tickets are the only thing I can work with! However, I will keep you in mind. If I manage somehow to book them for a decent price I will sell them to you face value.

I wrote to another guy who claimed to have four Ireland–Croatia Category 3 games. The face value price of these tickets on the UEFA portal are €30 a piece.

Me: You still have them cat. 3 ireland croatia tickets? How much? Please reply asap. Thx.

Tout 2 (Lynx): I have an offer from someone else for €80 each and to all 4 tickets that i have.

Me: I'll give you €100 for each.

Tout 2: Hi, Sorry for such late answer but i had exams and I had to study.

Yes I received some other offers and one of them will pay me €120 for each ticket for ireland–croatia game. Best regards, L.

Me: Ok, €150 per ticket. That's as high as I can go. Cat. 3 is crap enough in the first place. If you guarantee them to me I can send you this money in 5 days. J.

Of course, I had no intention of giving him a cent and the expletives I used in the following email telling him where to go with his profiteering are too x-rated to publish here. That was after he told me he had already struck a new deal for €120 per ticket from somebody else, and wouldn't sell them to me despite my higher offer.

So, even though I was also for the death penalty when it comes to touts, Martin showed the human side and made me think twice about the system that encourages people to be greedy feckers. I'd definitely mete out a much more severe system of corporal punishment to UEFA for allowing this happen. Martin may be on the lower end of this skulduggery, but still he deserves to be lynched.

So if you don't have a ticket, remember the following guidelines when dealing with a tout around the stadium or Fan Zone:

- **Befriend a Pole** – Ask him to pose as an undercover cop and bring him along.

- **Wait until two minutes before kick-off** – Then the touts will be chasing you, not the other way around.

- **Choose your tout carefully** – Avoid ones with scars, knuckle-dusters, amstaff dogs and wife-beater tops. Instead choose skinny, weak-looking and over-enthusiastic touts – you have a better chance at haggling with them.

- **Hang off your tout** – Prevent him from doing other business. Wear him down until he hates you so much he gives it for half his original price.

- **Play one tout off another** – Get them to win your custom.

- **Get your mates to pretend to be undercover cops** – 'Arrest' one of your other mates who is pretending to be a tout – then strike your deal fast with the real tout who'll want to flee the scene.

And most importantly, never forget the story of the legendary Conor Cunningham, the Irish fan with no ticket who travelled to Tallinn with a bunch of buddies from Cork and refused to pay €600 to touts outside the stadium. After failing to convince security they were with the media, Cunningham spotted an open door, explored it, got inside, found an Estonian tracksuit and a big bunch of footballs. He sat on the Estonian bench but got moved by security. However, they left him with his new gear, so he celebrated on the pitch with the rest of the Irish team after our 4–0 dream victory. All the time in his new Estonian tracksuit. And the moral of this story? Well, where there's a will there's always a way. And if you've got a big pair of balls, you'll get far in life.

iii. The sun and the beer

Without a doubt, the biggest threats to your personal safety and security this summer in Poland/Ukraine are … the sun and alcohol.

The weather doesn't take any prisoners in June or July and you'll be sweating like a fat slob in Penneys during the January sales. Hydrate well and carry water with you everywhere. Wear factor 130 to avoid getting sunstroke. Dust off and bring your best shades. Leave your old Salthill, Sandymount or Cobh bermudas at home and buy something nice when you get here. When the Polish sun shines, it burns Irish noses in about two nano-seconds and brings out long-forgotten freckles. The sight of pale legs among Balkan and Mediterranean bronze is a frightening prospect, so consider wearing fake tan for the first few days to prevent us from becoming a laughing stock.

Don't fall asleep in the sun while drinking, skinny dip at midday, drink vodka at the same rate as Poles or attempt to drink 70 per cent proof spirits before the big games. If you're found intoxicated under a bush, cops will bring you to a government-run sobering-up house. Kolska Street in Warsaw where the cells for drunks could be found used to be known as the most expensive hotel in Warsaw. Nowadays it costs a maximum €45 (250 zł) for a night – no breakfast included. Trust me, it ain't much fun.

You can be fined €25 (100 zł) on the spot for either drinking or having an open bottle of beer. There is also a night silence law in Poland – after 10 p.m. you are supposed to shut up, but they'll probably be fairly lenient during the championships. They know we are loud but harmless aul divils, so hopefully your parties won't see sight nor sound of the *Straz Miejska* or 'Municipal Police' (note: they have no powers of arrest).

iv. Prostitution

Some lads who come from Ireland to Poland for a party end up, at some stage, at a strip joint or brothel. Whatever your position is on prostitution, remember that Euro 2012 is about football and not about getting caught with your pants down and your wallet empty. Maybe you are a balding 50-year-old with a large nose, having a pint at your hotel bar. A young, local, blonde beauty approaches. Be realistic, take off your beer goggles, pinch and ask yourself this question – is this just too good to be true? It most probably is.

If you decide to travel further afield, it may also help to be aware that Ukraine has the highest rate of AIDS infection in Europe and the world's highest HIV growth rate. So follow the scout motto in Ireland – *Bí Ullamh* (Be Prepared) – and try not to get deported with your knickers around your ankles.

19. The Republic of Ireland in the Euro Championships

There's nothing worse than having to listen to some-body talk rubbish and get his football facts messed up. This is why having a quick and easy reference to check up on fixtures, previous Euro Championship results, winners, lineouts and so on can come in handy. When you have your facts straight, all you have to do is bet pints on the fool's assertion that Niall Quinn was the Irish captain in the last Euro Championships. See page 137 for some stats on Ireland's Championship history that might help win you a few bets.

i. Ireland's Euro 2012 qualifiers

Finishing second in Group B and qualifying for our first Euros in 24 years has been a tough effort by all involved. Let's jog our memories over fourteen months and twelve games to see how we got on the road to Poland/Ukraine for Euro 2012.

Armenia 0–1 Republic of Ireland (3 September 2010)

Birmingham's Keith Fahey scored his first senior inter-national goal after 76 minutes at Yerevan Republican

19. The Republic of Ireland in the Euro Championships

Year	UEFA Euro Championship record								UEFA Euro Championship Qualification record					
	Round	Position	Pld	W	D*	L	GF	GA	Pld	W	D*	L	GF	GA
1960 – France	Did not qualify								2	1	0	1	2	4
1964 – Spain									6	2	2	2	9	12
1968 – Italy									6	2	1	3	5	8
1972 – Belgium									6	0	1	5	3	17
1976 – Holland									6	3	1	2	11	5
1980 – Italy									8	2	3	3	9	8
1984 – France									8	4	1	3	20	10
1988 – Germany	Group stage	5th	3	1	1	1	2	2	8	4	3	1	10	5
1992 – Sweden	Did not qualify								6	2	4	0	13	6
1996 – England									11	5	2	4	17	13
2000 – Belgium & Holland									10	5	3	2	15	7
2004 – Portugal									8	3	2	3	10	11
2008 – Austria & Switzerland									12	4	5	3	17	14
2012	Qualified								12	7	4	1	20	8
Total	Group Stage	1/14	3	1	1	1	2	2	109	44	32	33	161	138

UEFA Football Championship – Stuttgart 1988

Year	Round 1 results	Goals
1988	Republic of Ireland 1 – 0 England	Ray Houghton 5'
	Republic of Ireland 1 – 1 Soviet Union	Ronnie Whelan 38'
	Republic of Ireland 0 – 1 Netherlands	

Source: UEFA.com / Wikipedia.com

Stadium. Robbie Keane had a goal disqualified for offside and hit the post. But a win's a win – a winning start was a key morale boost for the squad.

Republic of Ireland 3–1 Andorra (7 September 2010)

During the team's first competitive game at the new Aviva Stadium, Tallaght's finest product Robbie Keane potted home his 44th goal to secure a 3–1 victory. Kevin Kilbane opened the scoring by heading home after just 14 minutes while Kevin Doyle followed with a classy strike five minutes before the interval.

Republic of Ireland 2–3 Russia (8 October 2010)

Oh boy, will we ever forget! We trailed 0–3 after first-half goals from Alexander Kerzhakov and Alan Dzagoev and then, even more disaster – a deflected strike from Roman Shirokov. Robbie Keane grabbed us one back with a penalty and Shane Long reduced the margin to one but the Russians held on to claim an invaluable away victory.

Slovakia 1–1 Republic of Ireland (12 October 2010)

A hard fought draw in Zilina with a missed peno. from our captain. Sean St Ledger grabbed the first but it didn't last long as Jan Durica equalised before half time. McGeady was knocked by their keeper but a penalty save denied us the benefit of their goalie's foul. That seemed to knock the stuffing out of us and we ended up chasing our tails in the second half. Our next fixture would be five months away, so could we get back into winning form?

Republic of Ireland 2–1 FYR Macedonia (26 March 2011)

McGeady's first international goal after two minutes was a godsend and Robbie Keane secured a safe lead for us just before half time with a close-range strike. Our opponents must have known they were about to encounter the hair dryer treatment from their manager at the interval because when they emerged, they came at us all guns blazing with Ivan Trichkovski putting one past Keiren Westwood.

FYR Macedonia 0–2 Republic of Ireland (4 June 2011)

It was a night to treasure in more ways than one for our legendary captain Robbie Keane. After 8 minutes he bagged the opener and his second a half hour later wrote him into the history books. Keano had become the first Irish international to score over 50 goals for his country. Tricovski thundered a peno. against the crossbar soon after but the net evaded the Macedonians for the rest of the match.

Republic of Ireland 0–0 Slovakia (2 September 2011)

Automatic qualification was on the cards but, as history proves, our lads love to keep fans' hearts in their mouths. Given's fine display between the sticks was the stand-out performance but as a whole the team under-performed. In a word, we were crap. A draw worth forgetting.

Russia 0–0 Republic of Ireland (6 September 2011)

A record run of seven consecutive clean sheets shouldn't be surprising when you have a top class keeper like Shay Given in your ranks, but the scale of the attack on goal was so relentless, this away draw in Moscow could never have ended too soon. Dunne's momentous goal-line block denied Semshov and in the second half Shirokov failed to breach the mighty Dubliner. He almost single-handedly took on the might of the opposition and, in the process, picked up four stitches for good measure. His bloodied shirt had to be replaced with a makeshift no. 5 jersey, somebody drawing the number on it with a marker. A point away from home, we were now past the hardest parts of the group. So could we keep our focus and finish the campaign with two victories?

Andorra 0–2 Republic of Ireland (7 October 2011)

Kevin Doyle grabbed his second in the campaign while Aiden McGeady scored his second ever goal for the Republic of Ireland senior team. We were up 0–2 after 20 minutes, although we got a bit lucky when Lima deflected into his own net. But the cards didn't fall well for us. The Russians topped Slovakia, and the group was blown into disarray once again. Russia finish top of the table, so what next for us? Three points were a must to secure a play-off spot in our next game, and then what challenge awaited us?

Republic of Ireland 2–1 Armenia (11 October 2011)

Doyle's sending off in the second half put a bit of a dampener on Aleksanyan's bizarre first-half own goal. Richard Dunne netted home but then Mkhitaryan's goal ended Ireland's empty net record and more nails were bitten in the last 30 minutes than before a Leaving Cert. Irish exam.

Estonia 0–4 Republic of Ireland (11 November 2011)

The first leg of the play-off was held in Tallinn. Could we stay unbeaten for our tenth game? None of us I think dreamed what we were about to see – 1, 2, 3, 4... For Estonia, it was a nightmare – their two centre-halves got double yellows and were ordered off. Keith Andrews started our orgy of goals after just 13 minutes and we had to wait another while before Jon Walters, who turned out a great performance, matched it with a 66th minute goal. Our strike master Keano knocked in his 52nd and 53rd goals for Ireland, the last one a penalty, and you could already see lads checking flight prices on their phones to the various venues in Poland and the Ukraine.

Republic of Ireland 1–1 Estonia (15 November 2011)

In a sense, we only had to turn up at the Aviva. All the hard work had been done. But going down to Estonia in the second half was not part of the planned celebrations for our entry to the Euros, so thankfully the lads pulled it together and Stephen Ward helped maintain our unbeaten run of eleven matches. It was only the second goal in eleven matches that we had conceded and Trapattoni was oozing with joy afterwards and commented 'Greece won Euro 2004. With this group of players, why not? We have good options. It's not a dream.' 24 years is a long time to wait. I was just eight when Ray put the ball in the English net. So let's make a prediction and chant – 'Who put the ball in the Spanish net …'.

ii. Who is Giovanni Trapattoni?

When the FAI announced in May 2008 that Giovanni Trapattoni would be the new Irish manager, I couldn't believe it at first. In fact, I'm still trying to get my head around it. How did they manage to convince one of the game's most successful managers to take on mission impossible? I thought it was all an elaborate stunt by *Naked Gun* star Leslie Nielsen impersonating the famous Italian.

Hailing from the small town of Cusano Milanino, near the border of Switzerland, maybe it was fate that little Giovanni Trapattoni would find his way to Ireland, as he was born on St Paddy's Day 73 years ago. He appeared 284 times in the Serie A league with Milan and Varese in Italy between 1958 and 1972. Although he managed to score just three goals, his talent reportedly lay in stopping the opposition from scoring. He was capped 17 times with the Italian national side from 1960 to 1964 and scored one goal in this time, playing at centre-half in the 1962 Chile FIFA World Cup.

The Italian legend is known affectionately at home as 'Il Trap'. Since he managed to bring Ireland to the Euros, in dedicated fan circles he has gained cult status, being called more adoring names than Kim-Jong-Il, the late North Korean messianic dictator. I've heard him called 'Brilliant Leader', 'Shining Star of

Sugar Loaf Mountain' and – my own personal favourite – 'Ever-Victorious, Iron-Willed Commander'.

He seems to like taking on challenges, as he is also manager of Vatican City. Yes, they have a team. The Vatican Football Federation was set up in 1978 by Poland's favourite son, John Paul II, but despite divine intervention they haven't made inroads on the international scene. Trap is reportedly a fan of Opus Dei, the secretive Catholic society Dan Brown lambasted in *The Da Vinci Code*. His sister is a nun and he has no qualms about dedicating his success to the Almighty Creator. Given the closure of the Vatican embassy in Dublin last year, Trap is probably the closest link they have with the Irish people at the moment.

Of course, Trap is the man who almost got us to the South Africa World Cup in 2010. Some plonker called Henry screwed that up for us. In the 2002 World Cup, the silver-haired legend was over his home country's national side when they got controversially kicked out by a South Korean golden goal after dreadful refereeing, a wrongly disallowed goal and a sending off. But it is his record as a club manager where history will always remember him, being the one and only manager to have succeeded in winning all UEFA club competitions alongside the Intercontinental Cup (with Juventus).

Alongside Austrian coach Ernst Happel, he holds the record for having won league titles in four different countries (Italy, Germany, Portugal, Austria) is one of only two coaches to have won all three major European club titles and has won the UEFA cup three times. So you get the picture, right, he's hot stuff. Maybe that's why Ireland's very own answer to St Nicholas of Myra Denis O'Brien threw big bucks to woo him for the FAI. And this is the hard truth behind Trap's coming to Ireland as, without this, he'd be coaching Pope Benedict to run down the flank and how to score like Robbie Keane on his debut with Aston Villa. In his first two years over the Republic of Ireland, he is believed to have made about €3.5 million. In 2011 Trap signed another contract which will see him at the helm through the 2014 World Cup qualifying campaign. His new salary is understood to be in the region of €1.5 million per year, half of it funded by O'Brien.

The omens for Trap's connection to Poland are not so good, as his first defeat as Irish manager was in Croke Park against the Poles when we lost 2–3 in a friendly game. However, in his first major role as manager of Ireland, he managed to get us a qualifying place for the 2010 World Cup without suffering any defeats, setting another record to his long list. He also managed us to an admirable 1–1 draw with defending World Cup champions Italy, defeating them at the Aviva and to record a 5–1 victory over Estonia in the play-off for Euro 2012.

Ten years ago Trap reportedly carried holy water with him during all Italy's World Cup campaign – let's hope he brings rocket fuel this time round to keep the Boys in Green on the move and striking from all angles.

As Republic of Ireland's boss, up to the play-off with Estonia, he has had 42 appearances, winning 19 times, drawing 15, and losing 8. His club and international coaching career has spanned almost four decades and his record is quite impressive. He has been in the dugout, using his trademark two-fingered whistle, almost 1,200 times since 1974, winning over half of all his games. And with a loss rate of just 19 per cent, he is undoubtedly one of football's greatest ever coaches.

iii. Republic of Ireland Squad

Despite Giovanni Trapattoni saying he wanted to be loyal to the players who achieved qualification for Euro 2012, his rigid tactics and squad choices are being challenged by the great performances of up-and-coming talent in the Premiership. Impressive club performances by players like James McClean scored him a well-deserved place on the 29-man squad for the Czech Republic friendly. At the time of writing, the final squad for the Euros had not been announced; however, it seems likely to be the following:

Name	Position	Age	Club	Caps	Goals
Shay Given	Goalkeeper	35	Aston Villa	121	0
Keiren Westwood	Goalkeeper	27	Sunderland	8	0
David Forde	Goalkeeper	32	Millwall	2	0
Sean St Ledger	Centre back	27	Leicester City	25	2
Stephen Kelly	Defender	28	Fulham	29	0
John O'Shea	Right back	30	Sunderland	75	1
Richard Dunne	Centre back	32	Aston Villa	71	8
Darren O'Dea	Cente back/ Left back	25	Leeds Utd (on loan)	13	0
Stephen Ward	Left back/ Winger	26	Wolves	10	2
Shane Duffy	Centre back	20	Everton / Scunthorpe	0	0
Kevin Foley	Right back/ Midfielder	27	Wolves	8	0

Name	Position	Age	Club	Caps	Goals
Keith Andrews	Midfielder	31	Ipswich Town/WBA	27	3
Darron Gibson	Midfielder	24	Everton	17	1
Damien Duff	Winger	32	Fulham	95	8
Aiden McGeady	Winger/ Forward	25	Spartak Moscow	47	2
Seamus Coleman	Midfielder	23	Everton	4	0
Glenn Whelan	Midfielder	28	Stoke City	37	2
Keith Fahey	Midfielder	28	Birmingham City	15	3
Stephen Hunt	Winger	30	Wolves	38	1
James McCarthy	Midfielder	21	Wigan Athletic	3	0
Paul Green	Midfielder	29	Derby County	10	1
James McClean	Winger	23	Sunderland	1	0
Robbie Keane (c)	Striker	31	LA Galaxy	115	53
Kevin Doyle	Striker	28	Wolves	46	10
Shane Long	Striker	25	WBA	24	6
Simon Cox	Striker	24	WBA	11	3
Jonathan Walters	Striker	28	Stroke City	5	1

Source: www.wikipedia.com/www.fai.ie

Irish Player Profiles

Shay Given

Our World Cup 2002 hero has saved more great shots than I've drunk pints of porter. In 2005 and 2006 he was awarded the FAI's international player of the year. Born in Lifford, Co. Donegal, he has filled Packie

Bonner's gloves brilliantly and has been an Irish hero on many occasions, like in the South Korean/Japanese World Cup ten years ago. There must be something in the Donegal air that they keep producing such maestro net protectors. He is Ireland's most capped player and donates his international playing fees to charity.

Keiren Westwood

Born in Manchester, his grandparents hail from Co. Wexford. He has become a regular with Sunderland under Mick McCarthy and now Martin O'Neill. After many trials he finally made his break with Carlisle Utd and then Coventry city where he won the 2009–2010 club player of the year award. His crucial save in the final minutes of the Macedonia game was a godsend.

David Forde

A Galwegian by birth and former Galway Utd keeper, David won the FAI cup with Derry City six years ago. After some time with West Ham and Cardiff he found his feet with Millwall four years ago and has been a key member in their climb up from Division 1, with 20 clean sheets in their first season back. He also kept a clean sheet against Italy when we conquered them last year.

Sean Patrick St Ledger-Hall

From his name, it's fairly easy to recognise he's an English-born Irish player. and we can thank his Co. Carlow granddad for giving us access to him. From Peterborough Utd to Preston North End, where he spent five years, he has most recently become a regular with Leicester City at centre-half. But most importantly, he scored against the Italians when we drew 2–2 with them three years ago in the World Cup qualifiers. His defensive work impressed throughout the qualifiers and he is now a key member of Trap's successful team.

Stephen Kelly

After making his debut with Spurs and following this up with nearly 40 Premiership games in 2003, this Finglas right-back was Ireland's captain for the friendly against Uruguay last year. But let's roll back a little – he also played with Belvedere, Home Farm and Tolka Rovers before his move across the Irish Sea. He had stints with Birmingham and Stoke City before becoming a regular with Fulham from 2009. He made his international senior team debut versus Chile and took part in the Under-20's team at the World Youth Championships nine years ago. He captained the senior team in the friendly against Uruguay at the Aviva.

John O'Shea

A naive of Waterford, John had a very successful ten year club career with Man. Utd, winning five Premierships, one FA Cup, the UEFA Champions League, the FIFA Club World Cup and three Football League Cups. He has been with Sunderland since last summer but was put out of action by a hamstring injury, so let's hope he's in full flight for the Euros. Making his debut against Croatia eleven years ago, he was at the wrong end of Italian Giampaolo Pazzini's elbow three years ago. Bloodied but not beaten, O'Shea is tough as nails and a great assett for Trap's army.

Richard Dunne

Richard 'Put on more Russians – There are no more Russians' Dunne is from Tallaght. Playing for Home Farm as a schoolboy, two years after his international debut in 2000, he was part of the World Cup 2002 squad. At just 15 years old he started a five-year period at Everton, later moving onto Man. City where he spent nine years and made almost 300 appearances, scoring seven times. He has been with Aston Villa since 2009 and has scored nine own goals in the Premiership, a record we hope won't grow when he pulls on the green jersey this summer. With football legend Paul McGrath calling Dunne's performance against Russia the best ever from an Irish centre half, Richard is truly shining under Trap's management. Winner of the Three Senior International Player of the Year Award for 2011.

Darren O'Dea

Starting off with Home Farm, Darren crossed the water to play with Celtic as a youth and later with the senior team between 2006–2009. He spent a year on loan both with Reading and Ipswich Town, and after failing to find a regular pace with Celtic went on loan again, this time to Leeds Utd. He has played with both the Under 19 and Under 21 Irish sides, captaining the latter. He was a second half sub against Croatia last year and also lined out against Russia alongside Richard Dunne. He was recently awarded Three's FAI International Young Player of the Year Award for 2011.

Stephen Ward

Has also played with Home Farm, he moved to Bohs from Portmarnock, appearing 93 times while scoring

24 goals. Next he joined Wolves in 2007, setting a then record £100,000 transfer fee, and is contracted to play with them another three years. He's a former Under 21 and Senior B team Republic of Ireland player, scoring in his Nations Cup debut against N. Ireland last year. And of course he found the net in our second game against Estonia, helping seal a record 5–1 agg. win.

Kevin Foley

Both Kevin's parents are Irish (Co. Kerry), although he was born in Luton who he has played with since he was nine years of age. Twice named Young Player of the Year (2003–2005) he was also awarded Under 21 International Player of the Year by the FAI in 2005. Joining Wolves in 2007, he has been a regular at midfield and his good form has earned him a place at the club until summer 2013. Getting his call up to the senior squad in 2009, he played against Macedonia in the qualifiers last year and also N. Ireland in the Nations Cup.

Shane Duffy

The 20-year-old Derry-born Everton player is never far away from drama. The IFA (no, not the farmer's association) kicked up a fuss when he opted for the Republic. He underwent emergency surgery after seriously damaging his liver during a senior squad training camp collision. He has represented both Northern Ireland and the Republic of Ireland at Under-19 and Under-21 levels. Thanks to Richard Dunne's injury, he got his senior international squad call up for the recent Czech Republic game. One to be watched well beyond this summer's campaign.

Keith Andrews

A Dubliner who started off his career with Stella Maris, he moved to Wolves where he spent five seasons until 2005, becoming their youngest ever captain in a century at just 21 years old. He got nabbed by and spent four years with Blackburn Rovers after having great success as skipper for MK Dons in Division 2, before going on loan to Ipswich Town and ending up most recently with WBA. He made his international debut four years ago, scoring in our defeat to Poland. He has been a regular since the 2010 FIFA World Cup qualification campaign, netting a goal in Liege last year when we beat Italy.

Darron Gibson

Derry-born, Darron controversially opted to play for the Republic, which saw the IFA kick up a bit of a fuss. FIFA and even the Northern Ireland Assembly got involved, something the Good Friday Agreement authors probably never envisaged. In fact, he played with Northern Ireland at Under-16 level, but then went on to captain the Republic Under 19 and Under 21 teams. He lined out for Manchester United from 2005 to 2011, playing 31 times with the senior team and scoring three goals. Despite responding negatively to Trap's call for him to leave Manchester, in the end he moved to Everton earlier this year. He scored his first goal for the Republic of Ireland senior team in the Nation's Cup last year against Wales.

Damien Duff

Coming from Ballyboden in Dublin, Damien Duff won the Football League Cup with Blackburn and Chelsea, who he also captured two Premier League titles with. He spent seven seasons with Blackburn from 1996 to 2003, followed by three seasons each with Chelsea, Newcastle and his current club Fulham. Lining out in his senior debut for his country in 1998 against the Czech Republic, he was Ireland's Player of the Tournament at the South Korean/Japanese 2002 World Cup. He is hot stuff in Asia since his infamous bow after scoring against Saudi Arabia.

Aiden McGeady

Qualifying to play with Ireland through his grandparents (Co. Donegal), Aiden was brought up in Scotland where he spent three years playing with the Celtic youth side before breaking into the senior team from 2004 to 2010, appearing 185 times and scoring 31 goals, winning three Scottish Premier League titles. He's been with Spartak Moscow since then and is regarded as one of Russian football's top wingers. Despite first lining out for his country eight years ago, he only scored his first goal against Macedonia in our 2-1 win last year. Aiden was Eircom's Republic of Ireland Young Player of the Year in 2009.

Seamus Coleman

If you're a Gaelic footballer, then pay heed to this story. Lining out for his local side he was spotted by Sligo Rovers who he lined out with 55 times from 2006 to 2008, managing to hit the net just the once against Bray Wanderers. In 2009 and 2010 he was awarded the FAI's Under 21 International Player of the Year. He has lined out 50 times with Everton, scoring four goals. The

Nations Cup game against Wales last year was his first full international debut with the senior team.

Glenn Whelan
Starting off his football career with Cherry Orchard, Glenn spent three years with Man. City but only made one appearance from 2001 to 2004, before going on loan to Bury. He spent four years at Sheffield Wednesday, appearing 142 times and scoring 13 goals. Stoke bought him and he was part of their side who got promotion to the Premier League in 2008. He took part with our Under-20 team in 2003 at the World Youth Championships and has captained the Under-21s. Under Trap he has become a regular at midfield and who could forget his lightning strike against Italy three years ago when we drew 2–2.

Keith Fahey
In 2008 he won the PFAI Player of the Year award. Having started out as a trainee with Arsenal, Keith has also togged out for Aston Villa, Bluebell United, St Patricks Athletic and Drogheda United before settling in with Birmingham City since 2009. With Birmingham City he won the 2011 League Cup and with our senior team he knocked in his first goal after only coming off the bench in his first competitive international against Armenia in the qualifiers in Yerevan two years ago.

Stephen Hunt
Born in Laois, brought up in Waterford, Stephen used to be as handy with a hurl or a gaelic football as with a soccer ball. He previously played as a youth for Crystal

Palace then moved on to Brentford, Reading and Hull City. Versatile, he seems comfortable in the left of midfield, left back and is pacey and strong enough to be an attacking midfielder. He played for Brentford, Crystal Palace, Reading and Hull City before joining Wolves in 2010. In our 2–3 defeat to Poland almost four years ago, he hit the net from a penalty.

James McCarthy
A Glasgow-born Celtic supporter, he won the SPFA Young Player of the Year award in 2009. He has been with Wigan since 2009 and last year he signed a five-year contract with them. Since 2007 he has been part of the Republic of Ireland Under-17 and upwards sides, finally making his international competitive debut last year in the qualifier against Macedonia.

Paul Green
Paul's grandad is from Westport in Mayo, so the York-shire born and current Derby County player qualified and made his debut with the senior squad in May 2010. His seven-year stay at Doncaster Rovers from 2001 to 2008 saw him appear 277 times and hit the target 33 times while helping them gain three promotions. He scored his first goal in our 3–0 win over Algeria two years ago. His performance in our 3–2 defeat to Russia in the qualifiers didn't impress but despite this Trap called him back up to the senior squad for the Czech Republic friendly.

James McClean
The young Sunderland winger forced himself into Trap's squad for the Czech Republic friendly by his

impressive form. In August 2011, he signed a three-year contract with the English club and has shone as a regular under Martin O'Neill's stewardship. The Derry City born previously played with Trojans and Institute before moving to Derry City in 2008, scoring 18 goals in 73 appearances. He has been capped seven times with Northern Ireland's Under-21s but turned down a call-up to their senior squad to ensure his path to the Republic's team was clear. James is a very promising player whose form bodes well for the Euros and the World Cup qualifiers.

Robbie Keane
Robbie is the all-time record Irish goalscorer, first Irish player to score 50 international goals and is one of the 25 highest international scorers in the world. Our top scorer at the World Cup ten years ago, our second most capped player of all time, a member of the FIFA Century Club and the eleventh highest Premier League goalscorer in history with 125+ goals. Born in Tallaght just four days before me (he got all the footballing talent on offer), he started wtih Crumlin United before playing with Wolves, Coventry, Inter Milan, Leeds, Spurs, Liverpool, Celtic, West Ham, LA Galaxy and most recently with Aston Villa while on loan. With our national side, the trend is – when Robbie scores, we don't lose. So here's hoping his boots are golden this summer.

Kevin Doyle
Kevin comes from Adamstown, Co. Wexford. and is a former St Pats and Cork City player. He moved to Reading where he helped get them promoted to the Premier League in 2006. Three years later he

transferred to Wolves for a Reading club record of £6.5 million. He made his international debut in the same year as that transfer. He has played and is joint top scorer for our Under-21 team and was part of the Irish FIFA World Youth Championship squad in 2003. He won the FAI Young Player award in 2006, followed by the senior award in 2008 and 2010.

Shane Long

From Cork City to Reading, he was part of their success-ful 2005–2006 Championship squad, subsequently signing for West Bromwich Albion last year. Eighteen years ago Co. Tipperary club St Kevin's started nurtur-ing his raw talent and ten years ago he transferred to St Michaels. A seven-year stint with Reading followed where he made 174 appearances, netting 46 times. He scored in his Premiership debut with WBA against Manchester United. He has played with our Under-19 team and holds an interesting record – being the first player to play both international soccer and hurl-ing at Croke Park. He has been with the senior side since 2007.

Simon Cox

Teammate of Shane Long and born in Reading, he started off his road to international football as a nine-year-old with his home club, later playing for Brentford, Northampton Town and Swindon Town where he made 62 appearances and scored 35 times. He moved to WBA three years ago and has played over 60 times with them. He qualifies to play with the Republic through his grandmother and made his debut in the Nations Cup last year, scoring the last goal in our 5-0 victory against Northern Ireland. His brilliant performance against Armenia in the qualifiers earned him man of the match.

Jonathan Walters

A Merseysider by birth, he qualifies to play with the Republic of Ireland through his Irish-born mother. He found it hard to settle into a club and get regular football, moving from Blackburn Rovers to Bolton Wanderers, then onto Hull City, Crewe Alexandra and Barnsley. Back to Hull, he later played with Wrexham and Chester City but thankfully his transfer to Ipswich Town saw him play regularly, lining out 136 times and getting 30 goals. In 2010 he joined Stoke City for almost £3 million. He made his senior international debut almost two years ago and scored his first international goal away to Estonia in the first leg of the qualifying play-offs.

For details of the kits, captains, coaches and Boyle Sports odds for all Euro 2012 groups, see the photograph section. See Appendix for information on all Euro 2012 groups and player profiles.

Republic of Ireland Team Schedule

26 May: Republic of Ireland v Bosnia Herzegovina, Aviva Stadium
27 May: Pre-training camp, Montecatini, Italy
3 June: Transfer from Montecatini to Budapest
4 June: Hungary v Republic of Ireland, Budapest
5 June: UEFA Euro 2012 training camp, Gdynia, Poland

IV. Euro 2012 fixtures

Games below are in Polish time (take one hour off for Irish time).

Group	Date	Venue	Teams	Result	Kick-off
A	Friday 8 June	Warsaw	Poland v Greece		6 p.m.
A	Friday 8 June	Wrocław	Russia v Czech Republic		8.45 p.m.
B	Saturday 9 June	Kharkiv*	Netherlands v Denmark		6 p.m.
B	Saturday 9 June	Lviv*	Germany v Portugal		8.45 p.m.
C	Sunday 10 June	Gdańsk	Spain v Italy		6 p.m.
C	Sunday 10 June	Poznań	Republic of Ireland v Croatia		8.45 p.m.
D	Monday 11 June	Donetsk*	France v England		6 p.m.
D	Monday 11 June	Kiev*	Ukraine v Sweden		8.45 p.m.
A	Tuesday 12 June	Wrocław	Greece v Czech Rep.		6 p.m.
A	Tuesday 12 June	Warsaw	Poland v Russia		8.45 p.m.
B	Wednesday 13 June	Lviv*	Denmark v Germany		6 p.m.
B	Wednesday 13 June	Kharkiv*	Netherlands v Germany		8.45 p.m.

19. The Republic of Ireland in the Euro Championships

Group	Date	Venue	Teams	Result	Kick-off
C	Thursday 14 June	Gdańsk	Italy v Croatia		6 p.m.
C	Thursday 14 June	Poznań	Spain v Republic of Ireland		8.45 p.m.
D	Friday 15 June	Kiev*	Sweden v England		6 p.m.
D	Friday 15 June	Donetsk*	Ukraine v France		8.45 p.m.
A	Saturday 16 June	Wrocław	Czech Republic v Poland		8.45 p.m.
A	Saturday 16 June	Warsaw	Greece v Russia		8.45 p.m.
B	Sunday 17 June	Kharkiv*	Portugal v Netherlands		8.45 p.m.
B	Sunday 17 June	Lviv*	Denmark v Germany		8.45 p.m.
C	Monday 18 June	Gdańsk	Croatia v Spain		8.45 p.m.
C	Monday 18 June	Poznań	Italy v Republic of Ireland		8.45 p.m.
D	Tuesday 19 June	Donetsk*	England v Ukraine		8.45 p.m.
D	Tuesday 19 June	Kiev*	Sweden v France		8.45 p.m.

Euro 2012 Quarter-finals			
Thursday 21 June	A – Warsaw	1st Group A v 2nd Group B v ____	8.45 p.m.
Friday 22 June	B – Gdańsk	1st Group B v 2nd Group A v ____	8.45 p.m.
Saturday 23 June	C – Donetsk*	1st Group C v 2nd Group D v ____	8.45 p.m.
Sunday 24 June	D – Kiev*	1st Group D v 2nd Group C v ____	8.45 p.m.
Euro 2012 Semi-finals			
Wednesday 27 June	Donetsk*	Winner A v Winner C v ____	8.45 p.m.
Thursday 28 June	Warsaw	Winner B v Winner D v ____	8.45 p.m.
Euro 2012 final			

*Add one hour for Ukrainian time.

Source: www.uefa.com

20. Republic of Ireland v Croatia (Sunday, 10 June, 8.45 p.m., Poznań)

i. Who should we worry about?

Tottenham's **Luka Modric** seems to have fully recovered from his broken leg at Arsenal and needs to be tailed and closed down before he stirs up trouble. He caused a lot of problems during the Euros four years ago. **Milan Badelj**, who plays with Dynamo Zagreb, is a talented playmaker who links up well with Modric. **Krancjar** is their top scorer with four goals in the qualifying rounds so he needs to be watched like a hawk.

ii. Our history

We've met Croatia six times and the stats are in our favour. Croatia have won just once – and that was a 1–0 win in Zagreb in September 1999. We drew three times, managed two victories and both scored and let in seven goals. Let's hope we can keep this record on a winning streak.

iii. Memorable encounters

Euro Championships 2000, Republic of Ireland 2–0 Croatia

We opened our Euro 2000 campaign perfectly by defeating group favourites Croatia 2–0 in Lansdowne Road. Manchester United stars Denis Irwin and captain Roy Keane were the scorers. We finished one point ahead of Croatia in the group but one point behind Yugoslavia and failed to qualify for the championships with Turkey edging ahead of us in the play-offs.

Friendly match 2011, Republic of Ireland 0–0 Croatia

Five games on the trot without a defeat. Although it was only a draw it helped keep us on track to qualify for Euro 2012 and gives us an indication that we've got to up our game to come out on top on 14 June.

iv. Trap's nemesis

Slaven Bilic is a multi-tasker who used to be a power house player with West Ham and Everton. He could give our boy lessons in English, German and even in Trap's own language. He studied law and is supposed to be fairly handy with a guitar. He was a member of the brilliant 1998 World Cup Croatia team who fought their way to third place. He managed to get them to Euro 2008, their third time in the competition since they gained independence in 1991. Bilic's side are currently ranked tenth by FIFA, just below Italy.

v. Their championship record

Quarter-Finalist at Euro '96 in England but eventually lost out 2–1 to Germany. In the 1998 World Cup in France they were narrowly knocked out by the hosts in the semi-finals, before beating Netherlands 2–1 in the third-place play-off. Davor Suker was the competition's top scorer. They've missed out on just one Euro championships and one World Cup since 1991. In 2008 they finished fifth in the Euro championships

vi. Croatia's Euro 2012 qualifiers

i. Annihilated Latvia away 0–3
ii. Drew 0–0 with **Greece** at home
iii. Beat **Israel** 1–2 in Haifa
iv. Breezed past **Malta** with a 3–0 home victory
v. Good away win against **Georgia** 0–1
vi. Held **Georgia** at home to a one-goal margin 2–1
vii. 1–3 against **Malta** away
viii. On home turf beat **Israel** 3–1
ix. Lost 0–2 to **Greece** in Athens
x. Scored two home goals against **Latvia**
xi. Beat **Turkey** 0–3 away in play-off
xii. 0–0 at home to **Turkey**

21. Republic of Ireland v Spain (Thursday, 14 June, 8.45 p.m., Poznań)

i. Who should we worry about?

Well, hmmmm, all of them. Valencia's **Jordi Alba's** left foot is as good at crossing as Damien Duff is at weaving. He needs to be kept at bay rather than getting in risky supplies to their henchmen. One can only hope **Xavi** gets wooed and kept up by a stunning Polish woman the night before our game, or maybe overdoses on dumplings, feels heavy as lead and runs like a slob.

Barcelona's **David Villa** was Spain's top scorer in the qualifiers, netting seven times. He is also Spain's top ever goalscorer and his lust for more seems unstoppable. Torres, on the other hand, was dropped for their friendly against Venezuela in February due to his poor form.

And then there is the mighty **Casillas**. Even if it was our eleven against just him, we'd be happy with a 1–0 win. He's won every trophy in Spanish club football, the two biggest trophies in international football, and is still two years younger than me! 30 years young. Oh man, and he's still got at least another five years in him.

Casilla's is the only goalkeeper/captain to lead his team to both the Euro's and World Cup titles. With Italy's Buffon and France's Barthez, he conceded the fewest amount of goals by a winning team at a World Cup. FIFA's world's best goalkeeper in 2008, 2009, 2010. What else? Longest time without letting in a goal at international level for Spain – 120 hours. Eight clean sheets in the World Cup finals, just another two to equal the current record and three to beat it. Has a current streak of 411 minutes without conceding a goal in World Cup finals. The current record is 517 minutes, so Casillas has a chance again to break this in 2014. Oh boy, we're going to have to be firing on all cylinders to get it past this guy.

ii. Our history

We may have just won one out of our thirteen last meetings, but we can take some hope given England's 1–0 home victory in November 2011. We've played them 24 times, suffering thirteen losses, but we've also managed four wins and seven draws. We've scored eighteen times but conceded 48 goals..

iii. Memorable encounters

World Cup, 16 June 2002

Almost exactly ten years ago Spain broke our hearts with a 3–2 win on penalties in South Korea. With all the drama of Roy Keane's bust-up with Mick

McCarthy in Saipan, it wasn't a surprise that Spain went ahead in the eighth minute through Morientes. Ian Harte missed from the spot but in the 62nd minute Robbie Keane scored a last-minute penalty when Duff was knocked down. We dominated in extra time but couldn't finish them off. In the penalty shoot-out Matt Holland, David Connolly and Kevin Kilbane missed and Spain went into the last eight.

Spain: Casillas, Puyol, Helguera, Hierro, Juanfran, Baraja, Valeron, De Pedro (Mendieta 66), Luis Enrique, Raul (Luque 80), Morientes (Albelda 71). Xavi was an unused sub.

Rep of Ireland: Given, Gary Kelly (Quinn 55), Staunton (Cunningham 50), Breen, Harte (Connolly 82), Finnan, Kinsella, Holland, Kilbane, Duff, Keane.

World Cup Qualifiers 1989, Republic of Ireland 1–0 Spain

One year after Euro '88, Spain's Michel handed us a key victory for World Cup '90 when he somehow kicked the ball into his own net. Let's hope history repeats itself on 14 June.

iv. Trap's nemesis

He has a dangerous-looking moustache, his name is an intimidating **Vicente del Bosque** and he worked wonders at Real Madrid before taking over after their last Euro cup victory. Leading Spain to World Cup glory in South Africa in 2010, we can only hope there'll be another 34-year gap before they win their next Euro championship. And let's not forget, no team has ever won the Euro title back to back.

v. Their championship record

Spain are addicted to qualifying for the Euro championships. They are ranked no. 1 by FIFA and UEFA. Reigning but also first-time world champions. Currently Euro champions, their previous success was in 1964. They have a straight win record in the lead up to the championships, scoring 24 times.

vi. Spain's Euro 2012 qualifiers

i. A 0–4 away trashing of **Liechtenstein**
ii. Defeated **Lithuania** 3–1 at home
iii. Scraped win over **Scotland** 2–3 away
iv. Home win to **Czech Rep**. 2–1
v. 1–3 away win to **Lithuania**
vi. Breezed past **Liechtenstein** 6–0 at home
vii. 0–2 defeat of **Czech Rep**. in Prague
viii. 3–1 victory at home to **Scotland**

22. Republic of Ireland v Italy (Monday, 18 June, 8.45 p.m., Poznań)

i. Who should we worry about?

Antonio Cassano, well-known for having a short fuse, scored six times in the qualifiers, but we may be saved from seeing his best form as he is recovering from heart surgery and didn't take part in their friendly against the USA in February. Italy only conceded two goals in the qualifiers. Their defence is tight and the goalkeeper a legend. **Buffon** has been Serie A's Goalkeeper of the Year a record eight times, and if you can zoom back six years to the World Cup 2006, you may remember he only let in two goals and kept five clean sheets.

Mario Balotelli's increasingly impressive form with Man. City could mean he is a starter though he spent just twenty minutes on the playing field during qualifiers. Italy's coach didn't add him to the friendly against USA though due to fears about his lack of discipline on the playing field. So ideally, both Balotelli and Cassano would start but end up getting red cards against us due to their hot-headed play. 20-year-old Roma striker

Fabio Borini was called up to the Italy squad recently. His hard work rate and ability to hit the target with his club could see him flourish during the Euros. If Italy play against us like they did against Estonia we'll have to up our game. The Italians made 800+ passes in that 3–0 victory. Such free-flowing football will have to be closed down from the start if we're not to be run ragged. A few hard jostles, icy looks, smelly breaths, farts and jersey tugging may also help.

ii. Our history

We've nothing to fear when it comes to Italy in the Euros. Although the four times world champions have won seven of eleven meetings, we kicked their ass at USA '94 and in June 2011 Andrews and Cox secured us a 0–2 victory in a friendly at Liege. We've drawn and won twice and scored nine times against them, albeit conceding twice as many times.

iii. Memorable encounters

World Cup 1994, Republic of Ireland 1–0 Italy, New Jersey

In a World Cup that saw Irish players suffer terribly from the heat and humidity, Ray Houghton lifted all our spirits with a goal to treasure at the Giants stadium.

World Cup Qualifiers 2009, Italy 1–1 Republic of Ireland / Republic of Ireland 2–2 Italy

Iaquinta's goal suggested it was going to be a sad night in Bari, but Keano equalised from the spot three minutes before the end.

At home, automatic qualification was again in the pipeline. Whelan scored our first and similar to Keano in the first game, three mins before the end, St Ledger seemed to have edged victory for us. Up stepped Gilardino to win them a draw. And then we drew France in the play-offs. Grrrrrrr!!

Friendly match June 2011, Republic of Ireland 2–0 Italy, Dublin

On the anniversary of our last battle, can we repeat our victory? Our friendly at the Aviva stadium gives us lots of hope that we can build on our recent success and perform equally as well in the PGE Arena in Poznań Stadium. Here was the line-out for the game:

Republic of Ireland: Forde, McShane, Ward (Delaney, 90+4) St Ledger, O'Dea (Kelly 83), Foley (Whelan 60), Coleman, Andrews, Hunt, Long (Cox 60), Keogh (Treacy 75).

Italy: Viviano, Cassani, Gamberini, Criscito (Balzaretti 66), Chiellini, Marchisio, Pirlo (Palombo 46), Nocerino (Giovinco 59), Montolivo, Rossi (Matri 46), Pazzini (Gilliarno 59).

iv. Trap's nemesis

Cesare Prandelli was five years with Fiorentina before taking over the reins from Marcello Lippi's Italian side's with their brutal performance at the 2010 South African World Cup. Calling up Cassano has turned out be a masterstroke. His media-friendly style has led to his team being called *L'Italia del Sorriso* – Italy of Smiles. FIFA currently rank Italy at no. 9.

v. Their championship record

Nothing to be bragging about concerning the Euro championships as they only won once. They beat Yugoslavia in 1968 when they were hosts and it was the only major football final to be replayed. They reached the semi-finals twice and were finalists in 2000. They're the second most successful national team in the history of the World Cup behind Brazil, winning four titles (1934, 1938, 1982, 2006).

vi. Italy's Euro 2012 qualifiers

i. Secured away victory with **Estonia** 2–1
ii. Trashed **Faroe Islands** at home 5–0
iii. **N. Ireland** held them to 0–0 in Belfast
iv. UEFA awarded a 3–0 win against **Serbia**
v. Travelled to **Slovenia** and won 0–1
vi. Brushed **Estonia** aside at home by 3–0
vii. Scraped a 0–1 victory in **Faroe Isles**
viii. Defeated **Slovenia** 1–0 at home
ix. Only managed 1–1 away to **Serbia**
x. Slaughtered **N. Ireland** 3–0

23. What If We Qualify?

In the event that we come first or runners-up in the group, 1,800 km from Poznań to Donetsk or 1,068 km to Kiev is some road trip, but if you're up for it you'll be pleased to know that the Ukraine's hosting of the Eurovision a few years ago removed the need for visa travel for EU members.

You'll have a few hours delay at the border but there ain't any crazy Cyrillic script paperwork to fill out so don't worry. Just make sure you keep your boot locked on the way back in case some smart arse local decides to stash a few thousand cigarettes and himself where your spare tyre should be.

To check out the routes between the stadia, have a look here at sportmapworld.com/venues/euro-2012-stadiums.

The three other host cities in Poland and Ukraine that Ireland might have to play in are Donetsk (if we come second or get to the semi), Kiev (if we top the group or get to the final) and Warsaw (if we get to the semi).

If we get out of the group, you'll definitely have to cross into the Ukraine for the quarter-final, as we'll probably be facing either France or England. Many of the guidelines and tips already mentioned above also apply to Warsaw, and of course there are lots more when it comes to the Ukraine.

One key relief for fans is that since 2005 EU citizens can now stay up to 30 days as a tourist. So keep this in mind if you meet some strapping young fella or a blonde beauty and decide to prolong your stay.

Some key issues if we champion the group and advance will be: getting to the Ukraine safely and cheaply; arranging decent accommodation; sourcing a ticket that doesn't break the piggy bank.

i. Quarter-final/final in Kiev

Kiev is the capital of the Ukraine, has a population of 2.8 million and hosts two premier division football teams: Dynamo Kiev and Arsenal Kiev. The Kiev Olimpiysky stadium will see some great battles during Euro 2012, playing host to Group B, which includes France and England.

Getting there

By plane: Taking just one and a half hours from Warsaw Okęcie/Frederic Chopin airport, a return flight costs about €450.

By train: The no. 67 'Kiev Express' from Warsaw Gdańsk Station to Kiev Central Station leaves daily at about 10.39 a.m., 3.50 p.m. and 5.49 p.m. arriving in Kiev at 10.30 a.m. the following morning. You should book your marathon train journey in advance and get the sleeping-car with first class two-person compartments or maybe one of the second class sleeping-cars with four-person compartments. There should be food and drink on board, but have a back-up plan just in case. On the border there may be a couple of hours delay at Yagodin inside the Ukraine as technical work is done so the train suits their rail lines. You remain on board while this is done.

From Poznań you'll arrive at Warsaw Centralna which is under serious repair at the moment so you gotta get out to Warsaw Gdańsk station (*stacja*), 4 km north of the Central station. For updates on trains this summer also check out intercity.pl, pkp.pl and www. seat61.com.

Once you've arrived

Don't be afraid of the Orangemen – If you see a lot of orange flags, etc. you may think you've teleported to Portadown or the Shankhill Road. Eight years ago the Orange Revolution took over Independence Square in protest against alleged rigged presidential elections. Recently, one of the pro-western political leaders for reform, Julia Tymoshenko, has been imprisoned in what many believe was a political trial by her chief opponent. Anyhow, don't get too worked up if you see a lad in orange beating a drum. He's probably a harmless character.

Obolon beer – It's a key Ukrainian experience to taste this, or at least that's what my dad-in-law said when he came back from the Ukraine recently. It's high quality but quite strong so take it easy and pace yourself. Obolon's main plant here is the largest brewing facility in Europe, and the largest single beer manufacturer in terms of volume.

Family fun – Hydropark has infinitely long clean beaches, an open air gym, food and drink outlets, a bungee jump, beach volley courts, waterskis hire, wakeboarding. You could join the locals swimming in the Dnieper River. As always, take caution when wading or bathing in unfamiliar waters due to undercurrents, etc. It's a city river so keep in mind it may not be the cleanest. But it's a really great way to see how locals spend their free time relaxing.

Mystetskyi Arsenal – Once an abandoned military arsenal building in the middle of the city, it's now Kiev's leading arts and cultural space. 53,000 square metres in size it's one of the largest museums in Europe with art laboratories, libraries, classrooms and exhibition space.

Caves Monastery – Clare's Ailwee caves meet Glenastal. This fascinating place of worship for the Orthodox church requires you to carry candles to see the church relics, which are set in a maze of scary-as-hell catacombs. Kiev is the cradle of the Orthodox church that spread throughout Eastern Europe over a thousand years ago.

Guided tour to Chernobyl – This might be a far reach for you to manage, but there is a guided tour to Chernobyl, scene of the world's worst-ever nuclear disaster, 150 km north of Kiev. It's safe to visit for short periods and is something unique to experience while on holiday. I guess enterprising locals in Fukushima, Japan, site of a recent nuclear disaster, are already foreplanning guided tours there too. Try not to bring any glowing rods home with you, like Homer Simpson does at the start of *The Simpsons*.

The City Centre Hostel is Ukraine's one and only eco-friendly hostel. If the Swedes depart early you may be able to get a spot here. They can also organise tours to a top secret nuclear Soviet rocket base and AK47 gun shooting tours, the last option being something also a little unique to this part of the world.

Olimpiysky National Sports Complex – You can find it on the right bank of Dnieper River on the slopes of the city's central Cherepanov Hill in Pechersk Raion. Opened first almost 90 years ago, it cost €400 million to reconstruct and has a capacity of 70,000. Olimpiiska metro station will take you close by but unfortunately there's no link via metro to the airport.

Fan Zone – Kiev's fan area is situated in Kheshchatyk Street, and will occupy the entire Maidan Nezalezhnosti (this was where the famous Orange Revolution took place) and stretch to Bessarabska Square. Now there are lots of shops, restaurants, fast-foods, several malls and some public institutions. Also, there are at least three metro stations situated near the fan area.

ii. Quarter/semi-final in Donetsk

With a population of 1.2 million, Donetsk's motto 'Opportunity is proved with business' rings true when it comes to Euro 2012. Everybody has become an entrepreneur in this epi-centre of the Ukraine's coal-mining region. Odd as it may sound, the city's foundations lie in a steel mill and coal mines started in the area in 1869 by a Welsh businessman called John Hughes. UNESCO have awarded it the status of the world's cleanest industrial city. The English press have for months been talking about Donetsk as if it was a dump, but in fact it has its own unique qualities, which make it a worthy host for the Euros. Let's have a look at how to get there and what to do once you land.

Getting there

By plane: As the crow flies the distance from Donetsk is 1,600 km, so not really hitch-hikeable. Poznań to Donetsk with Polish LOT airlines passes through Warsaw, so consider taking a train there first. A return flight from Poznań is reasonable at €250 from 21–26 June (the quarter-final if we come first in the group is on Saturday 23 June). It takes three hours but there's a stopover in Warsaw for three and a half hours. It may be wishful thinking, but who knows. The airport is 8 km away from the Fan Zone

By train: See Kiev Section for the first major leg of the journey. Additional services are being put on and it'll definitely be no problem to get a train. Save a night on accommodation by taking a Kiev–Donetsk overnight train. They depart at 4.36 p.m., 7.23 p.m. and 7.42 p.m. arriving at 6 a.m., 7.10 a.m. and 10.54 a.m., respectively (these times may change so please check beforehand). There are first, second and third class sleepers, and for those who hardly have a penny to their name, why not jump on board the fourth class! So when you are book-ing or they are asking, you should know the following: first class – *Spalny Wagon* two-berth compartments, second class – *Kupé* (not to be mixed up with the Polish word *'kupa'* which means 'poo') four-berth compart-ments, third class – *Platskartny* open-plan dorm carriages. The Ukrainian railways website is at www. uz.gov.ua.

Once you've arrived

Match tickets – If you're not going by a ludicrously expensive quarter-final package tour, nor are a member of a club at home, chances are you're going to have to visit a tout once you arrive. As soon as you know we've made it, get cracking. Go to the Fan Zone and start asking. No matter how much you end up paying, just make sure you know exactly what the real ticket looks like (eater marks, strips, texture, etc.). Go onto polish-forums.com to see if any Polish people have tickets so you can bring it with you. The fact that they won't have the opportunity so late in the day is a good bargaining position for you. Alternatively, hang around until near kick off and hopefully there'll be people begging you to take them off your hands. And there is always the massive Fan Zone if that last resort fails.

Black Sea – The Sea of Azov is an hour away and as the world's shallowest sea might be well worth a visit if you have a few days to play with.

Donbass Arena Stadium – The Donbass Arena in the park zone of Kiev district, has over 50,000 seats, almost 3,000 places for VIPs, 196 spots for the disabled, over 1,150 media places and 45 commentary booths. The stadium's designers also did Man. City's and Bayern Munich's. You'll notice it's shaped like a flying saucer – conspiracy theorists can try figure that one out. Its two 92 square metre LED screens are among the biggest in Europe. Outside the stadium take a photo with the very cool 30-ton granite ball.

Fan Zone – It can be found in Sherbakova Park and is a massive 96,000m². It's nearby the main bus station and will be open from 2 p.m.–2 a.m. According to UEFA, there'll be football skill tests, five-a-side pitches, concerts and DJs. It has three huge screens and the capacity is over 70,000

Getting out and about – Vodka (*horilka*) with pepper is a staple drink in Ukraine. If you're looking for good beer, hit John James Huge's Brewery which can be found on Artyoma Street 129-B. It's a nice spot to chill out. The Park of Forged Figures behind Donetsk City Hall is an interesting place to put by a few hours. Social-ist metal figures depict lots of different things – Russian fairytales, soccer-related stuff, and well-known world sites. Chicago Biker's Bar have live music every night and I won't spoil it for you by describing how it looks inside. Just get yourself there.

Stuff yourself with local food – Their traditional food is in some ways similar to Poland and Russia, with *borshch* (beetroot soup), *vareniki* (dumplings with potatoes, cabbage or cottage cheese) and *pelmeni* (dumplings with meat). The restaurant at 3 Tolstyaka Street is popular for its savage food and reasonable prices.

Irish pubs – Golden Lion is in the heart of the city. It has live music and a great atmosphere. A nice dinner menu is also available and it is a great spot to watch the highlights.

iii. Semi-final in Warsaw

As the capital of Poland, Warsaw does not appear at first to be a city easy on the eyes, with its city centre blighted by an odd mixture of high rise hotels and business centres mixed in with miserable look-ing communist structures. Colossal advertisements

Warsaw National Stadium. Credit: Przemyslaw Jahr, WikiCommons

dominate building fronts and it's such an important transport hub you seem to levitate in between the crowds, rather than walk. But beyond this is a city filled with delights and treasures and one you should really stay a few days in to get a feel for. From the wild banks of the River Vistula, to the gorgeous Saski Park, its unparalleled nightlife and buzzing atmosphere, during Euro 2012 it's sure to reach unrivalled heights.

Łazienki Park – It took me a good while to find out why Warsaw's most beautiful park means 'bathroom' in Polish. It turns out to be a rather boring story to do with its palace, which is situated on a lake, and how it shows a bath-house from Greek writer Ovid's *Metamorphoses*. But it's certainly not to be missed. There are open-air Chopin concerts during the summer, you can pose for a pic. with free roaming peacocks, go on the pond with a paddle-boat for €2, see some open air theatre or generally just clear your head from the hustle and bustle of the city.

From the Old Town to Rondo de Gaulle – A beautiful walk through Warsaw takes you from the irony of what was the Communist headquarters and is now the stock exchange, past a Charles De Gaulle statue and an odd-looking palm tree on Jerusalem Avenue, down Warsaw's Grafton Street (Nowy Świat – New World), past a monument and church that holds Copernicus' heart, next onto Plac Pilsudski and the Presidential Palace, into Plac Zamkowy where you have nice views of the stadium just across the river and finally into the Old Town square where you can see the famous symbol and monument of Warsaw, the Syrenek.

Social realism – You will have noticed from your stay in Poznań and Gdańsk the communist-styled social realist architecture. It stands out as plain, functional, a little drab and dreary, yet also an interesting contrast to the glass-filled high-rise office buildings that intermingle with it. Many buildings throughout the city have worker monuments built into them, like at Rondo de Gaulle, Plac Konstyucji, the Palace of Culture and Science. Keep your eyes peeled for these reminders of the not-so-distant past.

Palace of Culture and Science – A gift from Jozef Stalin to the people of Warsaw to celebrate his birthday, it is now a UNESCO heritage site although many Poles, including the current Foreign Affairs Minister, want it pulled down. There is a viewing terrace on the 30th floor. It is also home to numerous exhibitions, a theatre, cinema and restaurant.

Warsaw Uprising Museum – Poland's first multi-media museum is really a must visit, as it's very hard to get a sense of Poland without knowing some key events that took place in their history and have forged their path ever since. You may have already seen Roman Polanski's Oscar-winning film *The Pianist*, so why not pay a visit and see how the Poles suffered but also fought back during World War II.

The beach – Close enough to the stadium and right opposite the zoo in the Praga district of the city is Warsaw's beach area. It isn't so big, but there is a cool bar, restaurant and outdoor volleyball courts that are always in use. At night there are often live concerts and DJs. A great place to meet locals and have lots of craic. Friends and family who came to my wedding had a whale of a time there.

Shop till ya drop – Well, you may not have much more disposable income but there are budget options for you. You'll no doubt see the wave-like structure of Golden Terraces (Zloty Tarasy) mall beside the Central train station, but the big brand names there can be bought at home just as easy. Instead, why not pay a visit to some smaller, uniquely Polish shops selling traditional clothes and souvenirs.

Hang out with a DJ Granny – If you are an old age pensioner soccer fan you may consider hitting the decks or the dancefloor alongside Warsaw's Granny DJ, 73-year-old Wika Szmyt. Otherwise stick to more popular and buzzing youthful clubs like Nowy Wspaniały Świat on Nowy Świat, Hydrozagadka on 11 Listopada Street in Praga.

By the River Vistula there are always outdoor bars on the banks. The capital is abuzz with great pubs and clubs. If it's laid-back joints (places, not spliffs) you're after then hit Lemon Cafe and Sheesha (Hookahs). If you are a fan of music from the 1970s and 80s then hit Mono Bar. Next to Metro Świętokrzystka and near Mono bar on Mazowiecka Street there are loads of other bars and clubs – Rich & Pretty, Zoo, Enclawa and Paparazzi.

If you're homesick, then pay a visit to the formidable Jimmy Bradley's Irish Pub in the odd location of the ground floor in Warsaw's Towers, near the Central train station on ul. Sienna 39. If you're a family guy/gal then hang around the beautiful Old Town district.

Giddy up in Słuzewiec – If you're a horse-racing enthusiast, then a weekend trip is to Stuzewiec Racetrack for a day at the races is just what you need. Place your bets, rehydrate with a pint and let the money roll in. Their website (sluzewiec@totalizator.com.pl) is only in Polish. It's called Oddział Wyścigi Konne Warszawa, Służewiec, ul. Puławska 266, 02 684 Warszawa, tel: 22 543 95 00. Call or email ahead to check what races are on.

Nowy Świat – In English that means 'New World'. It's in the city centre, quite near the Palace of Culture and Science. Ulica (Street) Chmielna and Foksal are among the most trendy places to hang out. There is an abundance of nice restaurants, bars, cinemas and shops around here. During the summer you can wine and dine outside while admiring the beauty of fellow fans and locals passing by. Bierhalle pub and restaurant, near Swiętokrzyska Street, is a good spot for home-brew beer.

Note: Given the nature of the draw, there is absolutely no chance that we'll end up in Odessa or Lviv in the Ukraine, or in Wrocław, Poland. That's why I've decided not to cover these cities in this guide.

iv. Survival Ukrainian

Pryvit/Vitayu – Hi/Welcome
Dob-rogo ran-ok – Good morning
Dob-ry dehn – Good day/Hello
Dob-ry vechir – Good evening
Na-dob-ra-nich – Good night
Do po-ba-chen-ya – Goodbye
Bu-vay-te/ Pa / Po-ka – Bye
Yak Spra-vy – How are you?
Yak vi nazivayetesya? What is your name
Ya pruyikhav z irlandia – I come from Ireland
Ya te-be koha-yu – I love you
Ya ne rozumiyu- I dont understand.
Garna pogoda, pravda? – the weather is fine, isn't it?
Meni pogano – i feel bad
Dopomozhit – Help
Normal'no – ok!
Spa-see-be / Da-koo-ee – Thanks / Thank you
Apteka – pharmacy
Kvytok – a ticket!
Bud' laska – Please
Chi vi govoriti po (angliyski)? Do you speak (English)?
Skilky koshtuye? How much is it?
Tak/Ni – Yes/No
De? Where is?
Yak doekhati do? How to get to?
Zdorovye! Slainte/Cheers

Numbers:
1. *odin, odna*
2. *dva, dv*i
3. *tri*
4. *chotiri*
5. *pyat*
6. *shist*
7. *sim*
8. *visim*
9. *devyat*
10. *desyat*

Here's a link to a basic Ukrainian guide drawn up by friends of mine:

http://doyouspeakpolish.blogspot.com/2011/12/euro-2012-survival-guide-poland-ukraine.html.

24. Final Top Ten Tips

1. Buy a Polish SIM card (in most shops) to avoid criminally high roaming charges. PLUS GSM (Vodafone)/T-Mobile/ERA/PLAY/ORANGE are all operators here and sell dirt cheap €1 starter cards then just buy credit for €1.10 (5 zł)/€2.20 (10 zl)/€4.40 (20 zł)/€11 (50 zł). You can also get ready-to-go starter cards that cost about €5–6 (20–25 zł). Depends on the network you go with, but it's definitely worth it if you are staying for a few matches.

2. Ring home with call cards (*tanie rozmowa*) on public phones (you need to buy a phone card (*karta telefoniczy*) to use the discount call card number - 0708 188 865) as it only costs €0.08 (35 groszy) a minute. The Irish code is 00353. Drop the '0' from the mobile phone number or county code.

3. You can only buy stamps for postcards/letters in a post office. It costs €0.40 (2.40 zł) to send a small letter or postcard to Ireland. You can find a 24-hour post office ul. Głogowska 17 at the Dworzec Zachodni Railway Station. For a stamp (*znaczek*) to

Ireland say: 'Prosh-eh zna-check doe Ear-land-ee'.
If you need an envelope ask for a 'koperta'.

4. Detailed maps of Poznań and Gdańsk can be found
    for free at most hotels and tourist offices. They'll
    also be able to help source accommodation for you
    if you are stuck. Find out more about Poland here
    with this interactive quiz: www.doyouknowpolska.pl.

5. Going for a pish – it's not like Ireland here, you can't
    just take a leak in the nearest pub. Public toilets can
    of course be found in the Old Town, Plac Wolności
    and at the Main PKS Bus Terminal and Central train
    station but if you're not a customer of a restaurant
    or bar they may charge you 2 zł. (€0.40). Big shops
    also require you to use deposit boxes so have a 2 zł
    coin handy. Tell them you have a party of twenty
    famished 120 kg males who'll eat them out of house
    and home later if they drop the fee.

6. Voltage in Poland is 230 V/50 Hz. They use two-
    pin plugs.

7. If you don't want to give up your seat to old
    women on public transport, close your eyes and
    start snoring.

8. Hitch-hiking is rare and a fairly dangerous type of
    activity given the state of some Polish roads and
    lunatics that drive on them. It's not as bad as the
    USA, where the rule is: If the hitchhiker isn't a serial
    killer, the lad who stops to give you a lift probably is.

9. If you are an a la carte Catholic and wondering whether to lie in or go to Sunday mass in Poland, then just snooze longer. You'll only end up sleeping during the one and a half hour ceremony anyhow. If you are religious though, then there are plenty of beautiful churches to visit in both Gdańsk and Poznań. Additional English mass services will more than likely be put on in the bigger churches around the time of the games.

10. If you are gay, bisexual, trisexual or asexual, pay heed to the fact that Polish people are quite conservative and aren't particularly fond of daytime public showings of affection even from heterosexual couples.

Republic of Ireland, UEFA European Football Champions 2012. Credit: Roberto, Creative Commons Attribution-ShareAlike 3.0 Unported license.

25. Important Numbers/Addresses

Embassy of Ireland
ul. Mysia 5, 00–496 Warsaw
Tel: +48 228 49 66 33; Fax: +48 228 49 84 31
Public office is open from 09.00–13.00 and 14.00–17.00.

Irish consulate
ul. Kramarska 1, 61–765 Poznań
Tel: +48 618 53 18 94, +48 501 43 21 44; Fax: +48 618 53 18 94

Emergency numbers
In the case of an accident or another emergency, please call:

Police – 997
Fire – 998
Ambulance – 999

For mobile 'phone users, the universal European Emergency Number is 112. Please note for the above number the operators may not have good English.
During peak season English operators are available: dial 800 200 300 from a land-line/public payphone or +48 608 59 99 99 from a mobile phone.

Poznań Taxis
Central – +48 611 96 61, +48 618 77 33 44
Express – +48 611 96 24, +48 618 48 04 80
Hallo Taxi – +48 611 96 23, +48 618 21 62 16, +48 601 21 62 16
MPT Radio – +48 611 91 91
Radio Taxi Lux – +48 611 96 62, +48 501 55 11 90

Gdańsk Taxis
City Plus Neptun – +48 581 96 86
Super Hallo – +48 602 31 91 91
Hallo – +48 583 01 59 59

Appendix: Euro 2012 Groups and Squads

Group A (Warsaw/Wrocław)
Poland squad

Name	Age	Position	Club	Caps	Goals
Łukasz Fabiański	27	Goalkeeper	Arsenal	20	0
Wojciech Szczęsny	22	Goalkeeper	Arsenal	2	0
Przemysław Tytoń	25	Goalkeeper	PSV Eindhoven	5	0
Marcin Wasilewski	32	Right back	Anderlecht	45	1
Jakub Wawrzyniak	28	Defender	Legia Warsaw	25	0
Tomasz Jodłowiec	27	Centre back/defensive MF	Polonia Warsaw	24	0
Łukasz Piszczek	27	Right back	Borussia Dortmund	22	0
Grzegorz Wojtkowiak	28	Right back	Lech Poznan	17	0
Arkadiusz Głowacki	33	Defender	Trabzonspor (Turkey)	29	0
Sebastian Boenisch	25	Right/left back	Werder Bremen	3	0
Marcin Kamiński	20	Centre back	Lech Poznan	1	0
Dariusz Dudka	28	Centre back/defensive MF	Auxerre	61	2
Jakub Błaszczykowski	26	MF	Borussia Dortmund	49	8
Sebastian Mila	29	MF	Śląsk Wrocław	30	6
Sławomir Peszko	27	MF	FC Köln	25	1
Ludovic Obraniak	27	MF	Bordeaux	21	4

Name	Age	Position	Club	Caps	Goals
Adrian Mierzejewski	26	MF	Trabzonspor (Turkey)	20	1
Maciej Rybus	22	Winger	Terek Grozny (Russia)	19	1
Adam Matuszczyk	23	MF	Fortuna Düsseldorf	17	1
Eugen Polański	26	MF	Mainz 05	5	0
Robert Lewandowski	23	Striker	Borussia Dortmund	40	13
Ireneusz Jeleń	30	Striker	Lille	29	5
Kamil Grosicki	24	Sriker	Sivasspor (Turkey)	11	0
Paweł Brożek	29	Striker	Celtic	32	8
Greece squad					
Alexandros Tzorvas	29	Goalkeeper	Palermo	16	0
Kostas Chalkias	38	Goalkeeper	PAOK	29	0
Orestis Karnezis	26	Goalkeeper	Panathinaikos	1	0
Giannis Maniatis	25	Right Back/defensive MF	Olympiacos	7	0
Iosif Cholevas	27	Left back/winger	Olympiacos	2	0
Nikos Spyropoulos	28	Left back	Panathinaikos	27	1
Avraam Papadopoulos	28	Centre back	Olympiacos	31	0
Vasilis Torosidis	27	Left back	Olympiacos	43	5
Sokratis Papastathopoulos	24	Centre back/right back	Werder Bremen	26	0
Kyriakos Papadopoulos	20	Centre back	Schalke 04	7	2
Grigoris Makos	25	Defensive MF	AEK Athens	10	0

Name	Age	Position	Club	Caps	Goals
Loukas Vyntra	31	Defender	Panathinaikos	42	0
Giorgos Karagounis	36	MF	Panathinaikos	115	8
Giorgos Fotakis	30	MF	PAOK	9	2
Kostas Katsouranis	33	Defensive MF	Panathinaikos	89	9
Giannis Fetfatzidis	21	Attacking MF/ winger	Olympiakos	12	3
Giannis Fetfatzidis	21	Attacking MF/winger	Olympiakos	12	3
Pantelis Kafes	33	MF	AEK Athens	40	3
Giorgos Samaras	27	Striker/winger	Celtic	52	7
Nikos Lyberopoulos	36	Centre fwd/attacking MF	AEK Athens	74	13
Stefanos Athanasiadis	23	Striker	PAOK	3	0
Dimitris Salpigidis	30	Striker/right winger	Dimitris Salpigidis	55	7
Theofanis Gekas	32	Striker	Samsunspor (Turkey)	56	21
Lazaros Christodoulopoulos	25	Winger/second striker	Panathinaikos	7	0
Angelos Charisteas	32	Striker	Panetolikos	88	25
Russia squad					
Vladimir Gabulov	28	Goalkeeper	Anzhi Makhachkala	7	
Igor Akinfeev	26	Goalkeeper	CSKA Moscow	50	0
Vyacheslav Malafeev	33	Goalkeeper	Zenit Saint Petersburg	23	0
Aleksandr Anyukov	29	Right back	Zenit Saint Petersburg	63	1
Vasili Berezutskiy	29	Defender	CSKA Moscow	61	2

Name	Age	Position	Club	Caps	Goals
Sergei Ignashevich	32	Centre back	CSKA Moscow	72	5
Yuri Zhirkov	28	Left back	Anzhi Makhachkala	49	0
Aleksei Berezutskiy	29	Centre back	CSKA Moscow	45	0
Yevgeni Makeyev	22	Full back	Spartak Moscow1		0
Roman Shirokov	30	Central MF	Zenit Saint Petersburg	19	4
Igor Denisov	28	Defensive MF	Zenit Saint Petersburg	23	0
Konstantin Zyryanov	34	MF	Zenit Saint Petersburg	47	7
Alan Dzagoev	22	Attacking MF	CSKA Moscow	18	4
Igor Semshov	34	Central MF	Dynamo Moscow	56	3
Dmitri Loskov	38	MF	Lokomotiv Moscow	25	2
Sergei Semak	36	MF	Zenit Saint Petersburg	65	4
Dmitri Torbinskiy	28	MF	Lokomotiv Moscow	26	2
Vladimir Bystrov	28	MF	Zenit Saint Petersburg	35	4
Dmitri Kombarov	25	Left winger	Spartak Moscow	1	0
Roman Pavlyuchenko	35	Striker	Lokomotiv Moscow	45	20
Andrei Arshavin (c)	31	Winger/forward	Zenit Saint Petersburg	68	17
Pavel Pogrebnyak	28	Striker	Fulham	31	8
Aleksander Kerzhakov	29	Striker	Zenit Saint Petersburg	58	17
Artem Dzyuba	23	Striker	Spartak Moscow	1	0
Renat Yanbaev	28	Striker	Lokomotiv Moscow	11	0

Name	Age	Position	Club	Caps	Goals
Czech Republic squad					
Petr Čech	29	Goalkeeper	Chelsea	89	0
Jaroslav Drobný	32	Goalkeeper	Hamburger SV	5	0
Michal Kadlec	27	Left back	Bayer Leverkusen	33	7
Tomáš Sivok	28	Centre back	Beşiktaş (Turkey)	24	3
Daniel Pudil	26	Left back	Cesena	22	2
Roman Hubník	27	Centre back	Hertha Berlin	20	2
Jan Rajnoch	30	Defender	Sivasspor	15	0
Theodor Gebre Selassie	25	Centre back	Slovan Liberec	8	0
David Limberský	28	Left back	Viktoria Plzeň	7	0
Zdeněk Pospěch	33	Right back	Mainz 05	31	2
Tomáš Rosický	31	Attacking MF	Arsenal	85	20
Jaroslav Plašil	30	Left winger	Bordeaux	70	6
Tomáš Hübschman	30	Central defender	Shakhtar Donetsk	41	0
Daniel Kolář	26	MF	Viktoria Plzeň	9	1
Milan Petržela	28	Winger	Viktoria Plzeň	9	0
Václav Pilař	23	Winger	Viktoria Plzeň	7	1
Petr Jiráček	26	MF	Wolfsburg	6	1
Marek Matějovský	30	MF	Sparta Prague	15	1
Kamil Vacek	25	MF	Chievo	6	0
Jan Polák	31	MF	VfL Wolfsburg	57	7

Name	Age	Position	Club	Caps	Goals
Milan Baroš	30	Striker	Galatasaray	87	40
Jiří Štajner	35	Striker	Slovan Liberec	37	4
David Lafata	30	Striker	Baumit Jablonec	16	2
Tomáš Pekhart	22	Striker	Nürnberg	9	0
Martin Fenin	25	Striker	Energie Cottbus	16	3
Tomáš Necid	22	Striker	CSKA Moscow	25	7
Jan Rezek	29	Striker	Anorthosis Famagusta (Cyprus)	12	3
Group B (Kharkiv/Lviv)					
Germany squad					
Manuel Neuer	26	Goalkeeper	Bayern Munich	25	0
Tim Wiese	30	Goalkeeper	Werder Bremen	6	0
Marcel Schmelzer	24	Left back	Borussia Dortmund	5	0
Benedikt Höwedes	24	Centre back	Schalke 04	7	0
Dennis Aogo	25	Left back/MF	Hamburger SV	10	0
Philipp Lahm (Captain)	28	Full back	Bayern Munich	85	4
Per Mertesacker	27	Centre back	Arsenal	79	1
Arne Friedrich	33	Defender	Chicago Fire	82	1
Mats Hummels	23	Defender	Borussia Dortmund	13	0
Holger Badstuber	23	Centre back/left back	Bayern Munich	19	1
Christian Träsch	24	Centre back/left back	VfL Wolfsburg	10	0

Name	Age	Position	Club	Caps	Goals
Jérôme Boateng	23	Defender	Bayern Munich	10	0
Name:Sami Khedira	25	MF	Real Madrid	25	1
Simon Rolfes	30	Defensive MF	Bayer Leverkusen	26	2
Mesut Özil	23	Attacking MF	Real Madrid	31	8
André Schürrle	21	Forward/winger	Bayer Leverkusen	12	5
Thomas Müller	22	MF	Bayern Munich	26	10
Toni Kroos	22	Bayern Munich	MF/winger	25	2
Marco Reus	23	MF	Borussia Mönchengladbach	4	0
Lars Bender	23	Striker	Bayer Leverkusen	4	0
Miroslav Klose	33	Striker	Lazio	114	63
Cacau	31	Striker	VfB Stuttgart	22	6
Mario Gómez	26	Striker	Bayern Munich	51	21
Mario Götze	20	MF	Borussia Dortmund	12	2
Lukas Podolski	27	MF	FC Köln	95	43
Bastian Schweinsteiger	27	MF	Bayern Munich	90	23
Netherlands squad					
Maarten Stekelenburg	29	Goalkeeper	Roma	45	0
Michel Vorm	28	Goalkeeper	Swansea City	9	0
John Heitinga	28	Defender	Everton	75	7
Joris Mathijsen	32	Centre back	Málaga	79	3

Appendix: Euro 2012 Groups and Squads

Name	Age	Position	Club	Caps	Goals
Khalid Boulahrouz	30	Defender	VfB Stuttgart	35	0
Erik Pieters	23	Left back	PSV Eindhoven	15	0
Jeffrey Bruma	20	Centre back	Club:Hamburger SV	4	0
Ron Vlaar	27	Centre back	Feyenoord	5	0
Hedwiges Maduro	27	Defensive MF	Valencia	18	0
Mark van Bommel (Captain)	35	MF	AC Milan	74	10
Nigel de Jong	27	Defensive MF	Man City	57	1
Wesley Sneijder	28	Attacking MF	Inter Milan	81	23
Arjen Robben	28	Winger	Bayern Munich	54	17
Stijn Schaars	28	MF	Sporting Lisbon	16	0
Kevin Strootman	22	Central MF	PSV Eindhoven	10	1
Urby Emanuelson	26	MF	AC Milan	15	0
Rafael van der Vaart	29	Attacking MF	Spurs	93	17
Ibrahim Afellay	26	Winger	Barcelona	36	3
Demy de Zeeuw	29	MF	Spartak Moscow	27	0
Dirk Kuyt	31	Forward/winger	Liverpool	85	24
Robin van Persie	28	Striker	Arsenal	62	25
Klaas-Jan Huntelaar	28	Striker	Schalke 04	50	31
Luuk de Jong	21	Striker	Twente	7	1
Ryan Babel	25	Winger/striker	Hoffenheim	42	5
Eljero Elia	25	Winger	Juventus	26	2

Name	Age	Position	Club	Caps	Goals
Portugal squad					
Eduardo	29	Goalkeeper	Benfica	27	0
Rui Patrício	24	Goalkeeper	Sporting Lisbon	10	0
Bruno Alves	30	Centre back	Zenit Saint Petersburg	48	5
Pepe	29	Centre back	Real Madrid	38	2
Fábio Coentrão	24	Wing back	Real Madrid	20	1
João Pereira	28	Right back	Sporting Lisbon	13	0
Rolando	26	Centre back	Porto	13	0
Ricardo Costa	31	Defender	Valencia	10	0
Nélson	29	Right back	Betis	3	0
Ricardo Carvalho	34	Cente back	Real Madrid	75	4
Raul Meireles	28	MF	Chelsea	54	8
João Moutinho	25	MF	Porto	40	2
Miguel Veloso	26	MF	Genoa	22	2
Paulo Machado	26	MF	Toulouse	4	0
Manuel Fernandes	26	MF	Beşiktaş (Turkey)	9	2
Rúben Micael	25	MF	Real Zaragoza	7	2
Carlos Martins	30	MF	Granada	14	2
Danny	28	MF	Russia Zenit Saint Petersburg	23	4
Cristiano Ronaldo (Captain)	27	Forward	Real Madrid	88	32

Name	Age	Position	Club	Caps	Goals
Nani	25	Attacking MF/winger	Manchester United	52	12
Hélder Postiga	29	Striker	Real Zaragoza	47	19
Hugo Almeida	28	Centre forward	Beşiktaş	40	15
Ricardo Quaresma	28	Winger	Beşiktaş	33	3
Nélson Oliveira	20	Striker	Benfica	1	0
Nuno Gomes	35	Striker	Braga	79	2
Denmark squad					
Thomas Sørensen	35	Goalkeeper	Stoke City	100	0
Stephan Andersen	30	Goalkeeper	Evian	8	0
Anders Lindegaard	27	Goalkeeper	Man Utd	5	0
Simon Kjær	22	Centre back	Roma	22	0
Daniel Wass	22	Right back	Evian	4	0
Lars Jacobsen	32	Right back	Copenhagen	49	1
Daniel Agger (c)	27	Centre back	Liverpool	44	5
Simon Poulsen	27	Left back	AZ	16	0
Andreas Bjelland	23	Centre back	Nordsjælland	5	0
Christian Poulsen	32	Defensive MF	Evian	90	6
Thomas Enevoldsen	24	Attacking MF	Groningen	11	1
William Kvist	27	Central MF	VfB Stuttgart	27	0
Michael Silberbauer	30	Central MF	Young Boys (Switz.)	24	1

Name	Age	Position	Club	Caps	Goals
Lasse Schøne	25	Attacking MF	NEC (Holland)	9	2
Jakob Poulsen	28	Central MF	Midtjylland	20	1
Christian Eriksen	20	Attacking MF	Ajax	21	2
Niki Zimling	26	Defensive MF	Club Brugge	9	0
Martin Jørgensen	36	Attacking MF	AGF (Denmark)	102	12
Nicklas Bendtner	24	Striker	Sunderland	46	17
Tobias Mikkelsen	25	Right winger	Nordsjælland	2	0
Mads Junker	30	Striker	Roda (Holland)	7	1
Dennis Rommedahl	33	Right winger	Brøndby	114	21
Michael Krohn-Dehli	28	Left winger	Brøndby	19	4
Nicolai Jørgensen	21	Left winger	Kaiserslautern	2	0

Group C (Gdańsk/Poznań)

See Chapter 19 for information on the Irish squad and player profiles.

Croatia squad

Croatia had their UEFA Euro 2012 qualifying play-offs against Turkey, where they drew 0–0 in Zagreb. They have a fairly wide range of players who scored a good few goals, so hopefully we won't be caught off guard while closing down the obvious assassins like Eduardo, Srna and Krancjar. The definitive squad had not been announced when this book was going to print, but the following is what we can expect to face on 10 June in Poznań. Croatia's final friendly games – 25 May 2012: Croatia v Estonia (Rijeka, Croatia); 2 June 2012: Croatia v Norway (Oslo, Norway).

| Stipe Pletikosa | 33 | Goalkeeper | Rostov | 90 | 0 |
| Danijel Subašić | 27 | Goalkeeper | Monaco | 3 | 0 |

Name	Age	Position	Club	Caps	Goals
Ivan Kelava	24	Goalkeeper	Dinamo Zagreb	0	0
Josip Šimunić	34	Defender	Dynamo Zagreb	93	3
Vedran Ćorluka	26	Defender	Bayer Leverkusen	53	2
Danijel Pranjić	30	Left back	Bayern Munich	42	0
Gordon Schildenfeld	27	Centre back	Eintracht Frankfurt	10	0
Domagoj Vida	23	Defender	Dynamo Zagreb	8	0
Dejan Lovren	22	Defender	Lyon	13	1
Ivan Strinić	24	Right back	Dnipro Dnipropetrovsk	15	0
Šime Vrsaljko	20	Right back	Dynamo Zagreb	3	0
Darijo Srna (captain)	30	Right back/MF	Shakhtar Donetsk	90	19
Niko Kranjčar	27	MF	Spurs	69	15
Luka Modrić	26	MF	Spurs	54	8
Ivan Rakitić	24	MF	Sevilla	39	8
Ognjen Vukojević	28	Defensive MF	Dynamo Kyiv	37	3
Tomislav Dujmović	31	Defensive MF	Zaragoza	16	0
Ivan Perišić	23	Attacking MF	Borussia Dortmund	8	0
Jerko Leko	32	MF	Dynamo Zagreb	59	2
Ivica Olić	32	Striker	Bayern Munich	77	15
Eduardo	29	Striker	Shakhtar Donetsk	45	22
Mario Mandžukić	26	Striker	VfL Wolfsburg	27	5

Name	Age	Position	Club	Caps	Goals
Nikola Kalinić	24	Striker	Dnipro Dnipropetrovsk	12	4
Ivan Klasnić	32	Striker	Bolton Wanderers	41	12
Mladen Petrić	31	Striker	Hamburger SV	44	12

Spain squad

Spain's defeat to England at the end of last year and their 2–2 draw with Costa Rica caused some rumours they were slacking off. I have my doubts, but at least it shows they are weak in certain areas. The big question is – how can Robbie get one or two past Iker Casillas? That said, set pieces seem to be their Achilles' heel. If we can get multiple deflections we might be onto a winner. And Carlos Puyol is an OAP, so maybe we can exploit that too.

The squad profile below consists of their most regular players and those likely to be called up for Euro 2012.

Spain's final friendly game is on 3 June 2012: Spain v China PR (Sevilla, Spain).

Name	Age	Position	Club	Caps	Goals
Iker Casillas	31	Goalkeeper	Real Madrid	128	0
Victor Valdés	30	Goalkeeper	Barcelona	7	0
Pepe Reina	29	Goalkeeper	Liverpool	34	0
Andoni Iraola	29	Right back	Athletic Bilbao	7	0
Gerard Piqué	25	Centre back	Barcelona	38	4
Carlos Puyol	34	Defender	Barcelona	99	3
Sergio Ramos	26	Defender	Real Madrid	83	6
Álvaro Arbeloa	29	Defender	Real Madrid	33	0
Raul Albiol	26	Defender	Real Madrid	31	0
Jordi Alba	23	Left back/MF	Valencia	3	0
Javi Martínez	23	Defensive MF	Athletic Bilbao	7	0

Name	Age	Position	Club	Caps	Goals
Thiago Alcântara	21	MF	Barcelona	3	0
Andrés Iniesta	28	MF	Barcelona	64	11
Xavi Hernández	32	MF	Barcelona	108	10
Cesc Fàbregas	25	MF	Barcelona	63	8
Juan Mata	24	Winger	Barcelona	16	5
Xabi Alonso	30	MF	Real Madrid	93	12
Sergio Busquets	23	Defensive MF	Real Madrid	38	0
Santi Cazorla	27	Winger	Malaga	40	4
David Silva	26	Attacking MF	Man City	55	15
Jesús Navas	26	Winger	Sevilla	15	1
Fernando Llorente	27	Striker	Athletic Bilbao	20	7
Roberto Soldado	27	Striker	Valencia	3	3
Álvaro Negredo	26	Position:Striker	Sevilla	7	5
Fernando Torres	28	Striker	Chelsea	91	27
Pedro Rodríguez	24	Striker	Barcelona	15	2

Italy squad

It can't have been easy for Trapattoni when we beat his home team 2–0 last June. Maybe he felt a little like Jackie Charlton when Razor Houghton headed home after six minutes for that glorious defeat of England in 1988. Over the past eighteen months the Italian squad has consisted of at least nine players from Juventus, Trap's former love child. So can Trap pull it off again, leading our side to outmanoeuvre the skilful Italians? The table consists of players who've played in the past eighteen months or may be called up late for the Euros. Italy's final friendly game is on 1 June 2012: Italy v Russia (Geneva, Switzerland).

Name	Age	Position	Club	Caps	Goals
Giovanni Buffon	34	Goalkeeper	Juventus	113	0
Salvatore Sirigu	25	Goalkeeper	Paris-Saint Germain	2	0
Emiliano Viviano	26	Goalkeeper	Palermo	6	0
Christian Maggio	30	Wing back	Napoli	15	0
Giorgio Chiellini	27	Centre back/left back	Juventus	52	2
Domenico Criscito	25	Left back	Zenit	14	0
Federico Balzaretti	30	Left back	Palermo	7	0
Andrea Barzagli	30	Centre back	Juventus	28	0
Leonardo Bonucci	25	Centre back	Juventus	13	2
Daniele De Rossi	28	MF	Roma	71	10
Mattia Cassani	28	Right back	Fiorentina	10	0
Alberto Aquilani	27	MF	AC Milan	21	3
Simone Pepe	28	Winger	Juventus	23	0
Angelo Palombo	20	MF	Inter Milan	32	0
Stefano Mauri	32	Attacking MF	Lazio	11	0
Claudio Marchisio	26	Juventus	MF	19	1
Thiago Motta	29	MF	Paris Saint Germain	7	1
Riccardo Montolivo	27	MF	Fiorentina	32	1
Andrea Pirlo	33	MF	Juventus	82	9
Antonio Nocerino	27	MF	AC Milan	10	0

Name	Age	Position	Club	Caps	Goals
Giampaolo Pazzini	27	Striker	Inter Milan	24	4
Alessandro Matri	27	Striker	Juventus	5	1
Sebastian Giovinco	25	Second striker	Parma	7	0
Antonio Cassano	29	Striker	AC Milan	28	9
Mario Balotelli	21	Striker	Man City	7	1
Giuseppe Rossi	25	Striker	Villareal	27	6
Alberto Gilardino	29	Striker	Genoa	47	17
Fabio Borini	21	Striker	Roma	1	0

Group D (Kiev/Donetsk)
England squad

Name	Age	Position	Club	Caps	Goals
Joe Hart	25	Goalkeeper	Man City	17	0
Robert Green	32	Goalkeeper	West Ham Utd.	11	0
Scott Carson	26	Goalkeeper	Bursaspor	4	0
John Terry	31	Centre back	Chelsea	72	6
Rio Ferdinand	33	Centre back	Man Utd	81	3
Ashley Cole	31	Left back	Chelsea	93	0
Glen Johnson	27	Full back	Liverpool	35	1
Joleon Lescott	29	Centre/left back	Man	14	0
Micah Richards	24	Right back	Man City	13	1
Gary Cahill	26	Centre half	Chelsea	8	2

Name	Age	Position	Club	Caps	Goals
Leighton Baines	27	Left back	Everton	7	0
Phil Jones	20	Defensive MF	Man Utd.	4	0
Phil Jagielka	29	Defender	Everton	10	0
Steven Gerrard	32	MF	Liverpool	90	19
Gareth Barry	31	Defensive MF	Man City	52	3
Stewart Downing	27	Winger	Liverpool	33	0
James Milner	26	MF	Man City	24	0
Theo Walcott	23	Winger	Arsenal	22	3
Ashley Young	26	Winger/attacking MF	Man Utd	19	5
Scott Parker (c)	31	Defensive MF	Spurs	11	0
Adam Johnson	24	Winger	Man City	10	2
Frank Lampard	33	Attacking MF	Chelsea	90	23
Wayne Rooney	26	Forward	Man Utd	73	28
Darren Bent	28	Striker	Aston Villa	13	4
Daniel Sturridge	22	Forward/winger	Chelsea	2	0
Jermain Defoe	29	Striker	Spurs	46	15
Peter Crouch	31	Forward	Stoke City	42	22

France squad

Name	Age	Position	Club	Caps	Goals
Hugo Lloris (c)	25	Goalkeeper	Lyon	31	0
Steve Mandanda	27	Goalkeeper	Marseille	14	0

Appendix: Euro 2012 Groups and Squads

Name	Age	Position	Club	Caps	Goals
Cédric Carrasso	30	Goalkeeper	Bordeaux	1	0
Mathieu Debuchy	26	Right back	Lille	3	0
Patrice Evra	31	Left back	Man Utd	39	0
Adil Rami	26	Centre back	Valencia	17	0
Philippe Mexès	30	Centre back	AC Milan	23	1
Mamadou Sakho	22	Defender	Paris Saint-Germain	5	0
Anthony Réveillère	32	Right back	Lyon	16	2
Bacary Sagna	29	Right back	Arsenal	32	0
Éric Abidal	32	Defender	Barcelona	61	0
Yohan Cabaye	26	MF	Newcastle Utd	10	0
Franck Ribéry	29	Winger	Bayern Munich	57	7
Mathieu Valbuena	27	MF	Marseille	10	2
Samir Nasri	24	Winger/attacking MF	Man City	28	3
Florent Malouda	32	Winger	Chelsea	74	8
Yann M'Vila	21	Defensive MF	Rennes	18	1
Alou Diarra	30	Defensive MF	Marseille	38	0
Marvin Martin	24	MF	Sochaux	9	2
Kévin Gameiro	25	Striker	Paris Saint-Germain	8	1
Olivier Giroud	25	Striker	Montpellier	3	1
Louis Saha	33	Striker	Spurs	20	4

Name	Age	Position	Club	Caps	Goals
Jérémy Menez	25	Winger	Paris Saint-Germain	10	0
Karim Benzema	24	Striker	Real Madrid	42	13
Loïc Rémy	25	Striker	Marseille	17	4
Djibril Cissé	30	Striker	QPR	41	9
Sweden squad					
Andreas Isaksson	30	Goalkeeper	PSV Eindhoven	91	0
Johan Wiland	31	Goalkeeper	Copenhagen	7	0
Mikael Lustig	25	Right back	Celtic	23	1
Olof Mellberg	34	Centre back	Olympiacos	112	7
Daniel Majstorović	35	Centre back	Celtic	48	2
Martin Olsson	24	Left back	Blackburn Rovers	8	4
Andreas Granqvist	27	Defender	Genoa	16	2
Mikael Antonsson	31	Centre back	Bologna	4	0
Oscar Wendt	26	Left back	Borussia Mönchengladbach	18	0
Jonas Olsson	29	Defender	West Bromwich Albion	6	0
Behrang Safari	27	Left back	Anderlecht	23	0
Michael Almebäck	24	Defender	Club Brugge	4	0
Emir Bajrami	25	Winger/MF	Twente	15	2
Sebastian Larsson	27	Right winger	Sunderland	39	5
Anders Svensson	35	MF	Elfsborg	126	18

Name	Age	Position	Club	Caps	Goals
Kim Källström	29	MF	Lyon	90	16
Pontus Wernbloom	25	MF	CSKA Moscow	21	2
Samuel Holmén	27	MF	İstanbul BB	25	2
Rasmus Elm	23	MF	AZ	22	1
Christian Wilhelmsson	32	Winger	Al-Hilal (Saudi Arabia)	72	8
Ola Toivonen	25	Striker	PSV Eindhoven	22	4
Zlatan Ibrahimović (c)	30	Striker	AC Milan	75	29
Johan Elmander	31	Striker	Galatasaray	63	16
Tobias Hysén	30	Striker	IFK Göteborg	21	7
John Guidetti	20	Striker	Feyenoord	1	0
Alexander Gerndt	25	Striker/right winger	Utrecht	8	2
Ukraine squad					
Oleksandr Shovkovskiy	37	Goalkeeper	Dynamo Kyiv	92	0
Andriy Dikan	34	Goalkeeper	Spartak Moscow	8	0
Oleksandr Kucher	29	Defender	Shakhtar Donetsk	28	1
Taras Mykhalyk	28	Defender	Dynamo Kyiv	25	0
Vitaliy Mandzyuk	26	Defender	Dnipro Dnipropetrovsk	19	0
Yevhen Khacheridi	24	Centre/right back	Dynamo Kyiv	8	0
Bohdan Butko	21	Defender	Illichivets Mariupol	7	0
Yevhen Selin	24	Defender	Vorskla Poltava	5	1

Appendix: Euro 2012 Groups and Squads

Name	Age	Position	Club	Caps	Goals
Yaroslav Rakitskiy	22	Defender	Shakhtar Donetsk	14	3
Artem Fedetskiy	27	Right defender	Karpaty Lviv	16	0
Dmytro Chygrynskiy	25	Centre back	Shakhtar Donetsk	29	0
Vyacheslav Shevchuk	33	Left back	Shakhtar Donetsk	20	0
Anatoliy Tymoshchuk	33	MF	Bayern Munich	114	4
Oleh Husyev	29	MF	Dynamo Kyiv	69	9
Ruslan Rotan	30	MF	Dnipro Dnipropetrovsk	56	6
Serhiy Nazarenko	32	MF	Tavriya Simferopol	47	12
Oleksandr Aliyev	27	MF	Dynamo Kyiv	25	6
Andriy Yarmolenko	22	MF	Dynamo Kyiv	18	7
Yevhen Konoplyanka	22	MF	Dnipro Dnipropetrovsk	16	5
Denys Harmash	22	MF	Dynamo Kyiv	4	0
Oleksiy Hay	29	MF	Shakhtar Donetsk	29	1
Maksym Kalynychenko	33	MF	Tavriya Simferopol	47	7
Andriy Shevchenko (c)	35	Striker	Dynamo Kyiv	105	46
Andriy Voronin	32	Striker	Dynamo Moscow	70	7
Artem Milevskiy	27	Forward	Dynamo Kyiv	43	7
Marko Devych	28	Striker/winger	Metalist Kharkiv	18	2
Yevhen Seleznyov	26	Striker	Shakhtar Donetsk	27	5